CPACE Content

Practice Questions

Mometrix
TEST PREPARATION

DEAR FUTURE EXAM SUCCESS STORY

First of all, **THANK YOU** for purchasing Mometrix study materials!

Second, congratulations! You are one of the few determined test-takers who are committed to doing whatever it takes to excel on your exam. **You have come to the right place.** We developed these practice tests with one goal in mind: to deliver you the best possible approximation of the questions you will see on test day.

Standardized testing is one of the biggest obstacles on your road to success, which only increases the importance of doing well in the high-pressure, high-stakes environment of test day. Your results on this test could have a significant impact on your future, and these practice tests will give you the repetitions you need to build your familiarity and confidence with the test content and format to help you achieve your full potential on test day.

Your success is our success

We would love to hear from you! If you would like to share the story of your exam success or if you have any questions or comments in regard to our products, please contact us at **800-673-8175** or **support@mometrix.com**.

Thanks again for your business and we wish you continued success!

Sincerely,
The Mometrix Test Preparation Team

Printed in the United States of America

TABLE OF CONTENTS

Practice Test #1

Multiple Choice Questions

1. When developing a vision for the school, which of the following sources of information is most critical to consider?

a. School, local, state, and federal policies
b. Past school performance indicators
c. Feedback from students, staff, and other stakeholders
d. Performance of similar schools

2. Which of the following represents the primary source of school funding in most states?

a. Allotments from the federal government
b. Grants
c. Donations
d. Property taxes

3. Of the following, which is true about multiple assessments of student learning?

a. Different assessment types access different skills and learning styles.
b. Students must be re-tested often or they forget what they learned.
c. Summative assessments following instruction are typically sufficient.
d. Summative assessments enable adjusting instruction as it continues.

4. Transformational school leadership has been found in research as most effective for modeling and encouraging staff development and self-improvement. Which of the following best represents the strategies of transformational school leaders?

a. They build school structures to encourage staff decision-making participation.
b. They take responsibility for everything rather than delegating duties or tasks.
c. They give teachers ample direction for making decisions instead of autonomy.
d. They take charge of determining school priorities to unite dissenting teachers.

Refer to the following for question 5:

An assistant principal analyzes student performance data for the grading period and notices that a class of students consistently performs well in reading and has not demonstrated growth. The assistant principal is growing increasingly concerned about the quality of learning on campus.

5. A school principal has reviewed assessment data and is concerned about the quality of learning on campus. Which of the following would be the best source of data for the principal to examine next?

a. Student survey data
b. Teacher survey data
c. Classroom observation data
d. Class size and student to teacher ratios

6. To evaluate teacher effectiveness in applying instructional strategies, school leaders need a working knowledge of student-centered, research-based teaching methods. What is most true about these?

a. The Socratic method is a useful, research-based strategy for delivering instruction.
b. Project-based learning requires technology integration in order to be implemented effectively.
c. Cooperative learning has been proven to be an effective, research-based instructional strategy.
d. It is necessary for teachers to utilize technology to deliver instruction in order to be effective.

7. Which of the following statements is true about a school climate in which students feel supported?

a. Students find resources and support are readily available to them.
b. Students who share multiple classes are more likely to form relationships with one another.
c. Student roles and responsibilities are clearly defined in policy handbooks.
d. Student feelings of support are not affected by interactions with adults.

8. The technology teacher informs the school leader that the computers in the computer lab are outdated and make it difficult to provide technology instruction to students. What action should the principal take first?

a. Ask the technology teacher to choose a computer model to purchase to replace the outdated computers.
b. Allocate money in the budget to purchase new computers for the computer lab.
c. Refer to the campus technology plan to identify the timeline for replacing computers in the lab.
d. Request a district technology support staff member to service the computers in the computer lab.

9. Which of the following best describes what school leaders should consider when identifying professional development for staff?

a. Individual staff members' goals are most important.
b. School goals and vision always take precedence.
c. Individual staff member and school goals are of equal importance.
d. Professional development is primarily for accountability purposes and goals.

10. Which of the following professional development activities would likely have the most impact on current teacher performance?

a. A self-paced book study program for all teachers
b. Online courses that teachers select and participate in at their own pace.
c. A four-hour in-person training conducted during the school year
d. A hybrid online and in-person six-week course that meets weekly for a cohort of teachers

11. Which of the following is true regarding how teacher evaluation standards should be designed?

a. Teacher evaluations should reference clear instructional standards to prioritize student learning.
b. Teacher evaluations should be conducted by school leaders with a single standardized measure.
c. Teacher evaluations should be based on occasional observation and avoid critical commentaries.
d. Teacher evaluations should play a minor part in important decisions about teacher employment.

12. The dean of students informs the school principal that discipline data shows that a disproportionate number of black students have been suspended from school for the first semester when compared to the general population of students. Which of the following represents the best action that the principal could take?

a. Identify a mentoring program for black students on campus.
b. Assess the school culture to determine if there are negative assumptions or beliefs that impact teaching and learning.
c. Send an email to teachers that no black students can be suspended for the second semester.
d. Identify teachers who should attend classroom management training.

13. A school leader is new to the community and attends a district school board meeting. In what way can attending this meeting best support the development of this school leader's beliefs about educational issues?

a. By displaying the diverse issues and viewpoints across the unfamiliar school district
b. By demonstrating the areas of disagreement within a school district
c. By allowing the school leader the opportunity to learn how to run school board meetings
d. By shedding light on differences between a school's vision and the district vision

14. Which of the following is the best evidence of clear and effective communication regarding the school vision and goals?

a. Stakeholders who understand the vision and goals can articulate them in their own words.
b. Stakeholders can memorize the school vision and goals.
c. Stakeholders offer suggestions for revision of the school vision and goals.
d. Stakeholders support the school vision and goals.

15. When schools and leaders implement the continuous school improvement process, which should they do *first*?

a. Establish specific goals for school improvements
b. Reflect on instructional and leadership practices
c. Implement strategies for specific improvements
d. Conduct needs assessments for their schools

16. How can attending district school board meetings most help a school leader who is new to a school and community in both informing the leader and promoting leader willingness to change positions or beliefs about educational issues?

a. By discovering how diverse the new school district is
b. By witnessing how school boards accentuate diversity
c. By seeing how school differences correlate to distance
d. By realizing how districts are managed just like schools

17. According to the National School Boards Association (NSBA), which of the following reflects an unintended consequence of the Healthy, Hunger-Free Kids Act (2010)?

a. School districts are not committed to giving students healthy nutrition.
b. Many school districts cannot afford the higher costs of new standards.
c. This legislation provides all funding for compliance with its regulations.
d. Students are going hungry because the regulations limit food amounts.

18. Which of the following strategies is most effective for communicating school and student success to families and the community?

a. Publishing a monthly school newsletter
b. Sending weekly automated calls
c. Sending letters home with students
d. Hosting monthly community meetings

19. The federal Supportive School Discipline Initiative (SSDI) issued a (2014) positive school discipline guidance package. Why did the US Department of Justice (DOJ) collaborate with the US Department of Education (ED) in producing this resource?

a. To make school discipline consistent with justice and correctional systems
b. To address inevitable student justice involvement by disciplinary exclusion
c. To ensure that Civil Rights Act titles prohibiting discrimination are enforced
d. To establish disciplinary practices to keep juvenile offenders out of school

20. Regarding how school leaders involve students appropriately in school improvement teams and processes, which of the following is true?

a. Planning school-wide forums is always a school leader's job
b. Some students have conducted school-wide survey research
c. Students have never participated in hiring any school leader
d. Students testifying in the state legislatures is against the law

21. A school leader conducts a data review and realizes that the school will not meet an important milestone in the action plan for accomplishing one of the school goals. Which of the following actions should be taken first?

a. Begin developing a revised action plan.
b. Communicate goal progress with the appropriate stakeholders to identify the barriers and challenges that prevented the milestone from being met.
c. Identify who was responsible for the failure and offer corrective action.
d. Host a community meeting to share an update with all stakeholders.

22. Which of the following best illustrates the connection between the school community and local employment trends?

a. A school begins to offer health care courses and training in response to a need for more healthcare workers in the community.
b. The school librarian partners with the neighborhood library to share resources.
c. A school sets a goal to increase the graduation rate.
d. A school increases the number of dual-credit college courses offered on campus.

23. Which of the following would most impact the success of a new teacher induction program?

a. Providing optional coaching sessions for new teachers
b. Assigning mentors to new teachers based on the seniority of the mentor teacher
c. Providing opportunities for collaboration and leadership development
d. The school leader facilitates all aspects of the induction program

24. A middle school principal wants to improve the quality of teaching and learning on campus on a continuous basis throughout the school year rather than only reviewing annual performance data and making changes prior to the start of the school year. Which of the following strategies would best help the principal to achieve this goal?

a. Assess students every six weeks using benchmark exams and use the data to adjust the instructional program.
b. At the start of the school year, administer a comprehensive exam to determine what information students retained over the summer.
c. Administer a comprehensive exam to students at the beginning of the school year, in the middle of the school year, and at the end of the school year and use the data to make plans for the following school year.
d. Require that teachers maintain portfolios for all students to demonstrate learning and growth over the course of the school year.

25. The dean of instruction is preparing to implement an online literacy program that the school district has just purchased. Which feature of the literacy program platform best aligns with the school's mission to use data to make instructional decisions?

a. The program assesses students' reading levels bi-weekly.
b. The program tracks students' growth over time and compares their actual growth to expected growth.
c. The program autogenerates reports of student engagement and sends them to parents.
d. The program provides all teachers and administrators with access to a data dashboard that includes all data collected through the program.

26. According to experts, which of the following is the most important factor in how school leaders evaluate their teachers?

a. Being motivated to evaluate teachers
b. Making time for regular observations
c. Making time for longer observations
d. Making evaluations discrete events

27. The leadership team of an elementary school has implemented a new math software program for all students in grades three through five. After three months of using the program, the students participated in a district benchmark exam and they showed little to no growth in math performance overall. What step should the leadership team take next?

a. Abandon the program because it is not effective.
b. Develop a plan for monitoring the math program at shorter intervals to determine its efficacy.
c. Reduce the number of students using the math program.
d. Increase the amount of time that students use the program.

28. In many public-school districts, students with certain linguistic and/or cultural backgrounds are disproportionately enrolled in special education programs. How can a school leader best address this type of overrepresentation?

a. Examine current school procedures for assigning grade levels to students.
b. Examine instructional strategies targeting students referred to special education.
c. Examine instruments used to evaluate student need for special education.
d. Examine the curriculum and related expectations of student achievement.

29. Which of the following is true regarding best practices for school leaders when giving teachers observational feedback?

a. Leaders should give feedback statements rather than asking questions.
b. Leaders should disregard strengths to focus on improving weaknesses.
c. Leaders should emphasize all identified areas for improvement equally.
d. Leaders should include some specific next steps attainable for teachers.

30. Which of the following actions best exemplifies a focus on school-wide rigorous curriculum and standards-based instruction?

a. Increase the number of advanced placement and dual credit courses offered on the master schedule.
b. Increase the number of students taking college entrance exams.
c. Evaluate campus-based assessments for alignment to the standards and curriculum and revise where appropriate.
d. Offer after-school tutorials for students who are falling behind.

31. A principal notices that even though teachers actively participate in professional development throughout the school year, there seems to be little evidence of changes in instructional practices on campus. Which of the following questions best addresses the concern of the principal?

a. What is the process for giving feedback on the efficacy of professional development offered to teachers?
b. Are professional development sessions aligned to the curriculum, instruction, and programs of this campus?
c. How much does professional development impact the school budget?
d. How can I make time in my schedule to attend professional development sessions with the teachers?

32. A school leader is developing a process for continuous improvement on campus. Which of the following actions should the school leader take first?

a. Develop evaluation procedures and set checkpoints for evaluation.
b. Train staff on the continuous improvement process.
c. Select a low performing area that needs to be addressed.
d. Identify strategies for addressing low performing areas.

33. According to research findings, transformational school leaders are most effective in promoting organizational learning. Which of the following best reflects how they do this?

a. By demonstrating their high expectations for students
b. By demonstrating their high expectations for teachers
c. By modeling ongoing learning and providing opportunities for staff to learn from peers
d. By researching effective instructional practices and training staff to implement them

34. A school leader surveys key stakeholders regarding the school vision and goals to learn what they believe about the purposes of education. Which set of stakeholder groups is the leader LEAST likely to survey about this particular topic?

a. Superintendent, central office administrators
b. Members of school board, parents of students
c. Community business owners, business workers
d. Students, teachers, paraprofessionals at school

35. Which of the following should school principals primarily look for when observing teachers in classrooms for evaluation purposes?

a. They should focus on what students want to learn rather than what they want them to learn.
b. They should look for how comfortable the teacher is with the lesson content and method of delivery.
c. They should look for evidence of learning such as student responses to checks for understanding and student work products.
d. They should focus on physical classroom setup.

36. What is most true about effective new teacher induction programs?

a. They should focus on supporting new teachers but not leaders.
b. They should give only new teachers professional development.
c. They should use self-assessments and reflection for teachers to measure performance.
d. They should improve student achievement via teacher efficacy.

37. At the midway point of the school year, the school leader is surprised to find that the school is not on track to achieve the school goals for the year. What could the school leader have done to prevent being surprised by this information?

a. Established a plan for assessing and monitoring progress at regular intervals.
b. Delegated responsibilities to the leadership team.
c. Communicated the goals more effectively to stakeholders.
d. Created a committee to engage with the leader in the development of the goals.

38. A high school principal is concerned that ninth-grade students who read below grade level are not performing well on benchmark tests in reading and writing. Which of the following steps should the principal take to best address this concern?

a. Provide test preparation sessions for these students after school and on weekends and monitor student attendance to the sessions.
b. Integrate reading and writing skills into all subject areas and provide training to all teachers on fundamental reading strategies.
c. Increase the opportunities that students have to spend in the school library.
d. Purchase a reading software program that students can use at home.

39. Which is a practice that national research studies find school leaders should *avoid* when speaking publicly and in other communication with key stakeholders?

a. Taking advantage of the political environment
b. Using commonly understood language with most audiences
c. Communicating in response to sensitive situations
d. Becoming engaged in large scale open forums

40. Which of the following actions is NOT an example of a school leader functioning as an instrument of social justice?

a. Writing a letter to the State Board of Education regarding education funding
b. Participating in a community rally to protest the construction of a railroad through the neighborhood
c. Becoming a paid member of an education organization for urban school leaders
d. Campaigning in the school cafeteria for a political candidate in an upcoming election

41. Which of these is true regarding school leader efforts involving school improvement plans, policies, and structures to improve parent engagement, student engagement, and student achievement?

a. School improvement plans increased parental meeting attendance but not student school attendance.
b. School improvement plans decreased student behavior problems while increasing their achievement.
c. Central office policies and structures increased parent engagement in individual schools, not systems.
d. School improvement plans increased student enrollment and achievement, not parent involvement.

42. What is most accurate regarding social and emotional learning (SEL) programs that schools often offer in conjunction with school-wide positive behavior support (SPBS) programs?

a. Programming is implemented at individual grade levels
b. Programming requires quarterly monitoring
c. Programming includes practicing opportunities
d. Programming is limited to the school environment

43. A school leader unveiled the new school vision and goals for the academic year at a community meeting. Several parents and community members were not pleased with the presentation and were vocal in their opposition of the leader's plan. Which of the following was the most likely cause of poor community support for the school vision and goals?

a. The vision and goals were not aligned.
b. The goals were not rigorous enough to meet state and federal accountability standards.
c. Stakeholders were not included in the development of the vison and goals.
d. The community members do not support the school leader.

44. Which of the following criteria would make a school the best candidate for implementing an integrated management system as new technology for managing school operations?

a. The school has not been using any digital management system.
b. The school has been using one management system with no plans for more.
c. The school has one or more systems and plans on adding more systems.
d. The school wants separate system policies and documentation.

45. Among challenges that school leaders face in their efforts to promote student mental health, which of the following descriptions most represents the category of limited resources?

a. Accountability law has shifted school counselors' duties from mental health to academic achievement.
b. Prevention and promotion can address most student issues, yet costly treatments are routinely prescribed.
c. The mental health resources available to public schools are not provided proportionately or equitably.
d. Owing to our society's cultural traditions, the priority of mental health issues in schools is marginalized.

46. Educational research into collaborative data analysis has identified four areas. Which of these areas involves the process of exploring learning standards, goals, and definitions?

a. Calibration
b. Student data focus
c. Educator engagement
d. Supportive technology

47. Which of the following actions best demonstrates that a principal makes decisions to improve instruction based on evidence from student data?

a. Meeting with parents frequently during grading periods
b. Conducting meetings for Professional Learning Committees based on grade levels and subject areas
c. Requiring teachers to host tutorial sessions for students after the regular school day
d. Submitting reports to district office personnel after each grading period

48. A middle school principal has been informed that there will be a cut in the school budget in the area of technology capital for the upcoming school year. Based on this information, which of the following represents the best action that the school principal could take?

a. Do not offer a technology class for students for the upcoming school year.
b. Assess the current technology on campus and determine how to use current assets for next school year's instruction.
c. Apply for local grants to compensate for the budget cut.
d. Ask the community for donations of technology equipment.

49. All of the following demonstrate that the school leader conducts self-reflection EXCEPT:

a. Reading books and articles related to the field of education and leadership practice
b. Keeping a journal
c. Evaluating one's self using the personnel evaluation rubric
d. Attending a mandated training

50. A group of parents expressed concern to the school leader that they did not feel involved in the decision-making processes at the school. Which of the following actions could the school leader take to address their concerns?

a. Place a suggestion box in the front office of the school.
b. Create a parent focus group.
c. Invite parents to register as volunteers at the school.
d. Create an email newsletter to distribute to parents monthly.

51. In reference to the Supportive School Discipline Initiative (SSDI), former US Attorney General Eric Holder said a federal initiative to guide school disciplinary practices would "make schools safe, supportive and inclusive for all students" and would "keep America's young people safe and on the right path." How did he say it would do these things?

a. By making discipline less exclusionary
b. By divorcing discipline from civil rights
c. By getting data from resource officers
d. By referring discipline to peace officers

52. When using student outcome data to monitor school improvement progress, which of these would indicate a need to update the school improvement plan?

a. Data show improvement goals taking longer to be met than planned.
b. Data show that the school is on target to meet expected goals.
c. Data can be monitored more frequently due to acquisition of improved technology applications.
d. Data show that the school lags behind other schools with similar student populations.

53. The Tripod Project and other research-based initiatives to close achievement gaps have identified aspects of student engagement. For example, when teachers help them consolidate new learning, students are prepared for the future. Among other aspects, which of the following opposing pairs described as leading to success or failure is incorrect?

a. Trust and interest versus mistrust and disinterest
b. Autonomy of students versus control by teachers
c. Ambition in learning versus. ambivalence toward it
d. Industry versus disengagement or discouragement

54. A school leader has recently been appointed to school principal of ABC Elementary School. Which of the following actions would best help the new principal learn more about the community that the school serves?

a. Research the community online.
b. Review student demographic and academic performance data.
c. Meet with a variety of stakeholders of the community.
d. Meet with current staff to ask questions about the community.

55. Which of the following is an example of a community partnership?

a. Student club members pick up litter in the community on the weekends.
b. A local business sets up a table at parent meetings to inform parents about their services.
c. Local businesses provide mentors to students in the areas of business and entrepreneurship.
d. The principal invites a local business owner as a guest speaker for a teacher in-service.

56. Which of the following best describes the relationship between school leadership and student outcomes?

a. School leadership is directly related to student outcomes.
b. School leadership is indirectly related to student outcomes.
c. School leadership is not related to student outcomes.
d. There is not enough research to determine the nature of the relationship.

57. Which of the following represents a principle informing school leader support and professional development (PD) of teachers throughout their careers?

a. PD must be continuing and supported by repetition and follow-up to change teaching over time.
b. PD for teachers should be focused on practice and not on theoretical bases.
c. PD is best administered as a stand-alone process within individual schools.
d. When school leaders furnish PD, they should be sure to include the newest, most popular topics.

58. A school leader is looking to incorporate daily effort into professional development in a collaborative way across the campus. Which of the following professional development and learning opportunities is NOT collaborative in nature and useful for daily teacher activities?

a. Conducting action research
b. Professional learning communities (PLCs)
c. Daily reading of professional research in journal publications
d. Structured observations

59. Which of the following factors should a school leader consider first when scheduling a meeting with a large group of parents?

a. The languages that the parents speak
b. The availability of funds to serve refreshments
c. The day of the week and time of the day to host the meeting
d. The school leader's schedule

60. Which of the following is the best evidence of effective monitoring of progress toward the vision and goals?

a. The leader implements clear checkpoints and milestones for goal activities.
b. The leader provides regular updates to stakeholders regarding progress toward the vision and goals.
c. Student performance data shows evidence of growth.
d. An advisory committee meets regularly to provide feedback to the leader regarding the vision and goals.

61. Among classroom assessment principles that school leaders must know for effective collaboration with teachers, which choice is MOST representative?

a. A few specific assessment instruments are error free.
b. Authors and users typically overestimate testing error.
c. Assessment reliability applies to tests, not test scores.
d. Good assessment is valid, reliable, ethical, and fair.

62. A group of teachers who are unhappy with some of the policies on campus have organized into an informal group. They have begun inviting other teachers and staff to meet with them to discuss campus concerns. The school leader has become aware of the group. Which of the following is the best response to the formation of this group?

a. Invite the group to meet with the school leader to discuss their concerns.
b. Create a new campus policy banning the formation of groups without permission.
c. Administer a survey to the staff to gather their opinions about campus policies.
d. Require that the group only meet off campus outside of school hours.

63. Which of the following activities would not be evidence that all students are being prepared for and have access to a challenging curriculum?

a. Students who were enrolled in pre-advanced placement courses in middle school are automatically enrolled in advanced placement courses in high school.
b. The school leader regularly monitors student performance data on tests and in classes to determine alignment of campus-based assessment to standardized assessment.
c. All students are administered college entrance exams on the school campus at no cost to the student.
d. Students who have a history of meeting satisfactory performance standards on standardized tests are offered enrichment courses to help them reach mastery performance levels.

64. Which choice accurately reflects the school leader's role regarding laws protecting student rights to privacy and confidentiality of their educational records?

a. School leaders are responsible for knowing these rights but not enforcing them.
b. School leaders are responsible to enforce these but need not know exceptions.
c. School leaders are responsible for third-party disclosure but not written consent.
d. School leaders are responsible for policy on non-student and parent records access.

65. According to multiple research studies, what is a characteristic of school leaders related to evaluating teacher effectiveness?

a. The most effective school leaders are better at identifying the best candidates for hiring as teachers.
b. The most effective school leaders are better at identifying the best and worst teachers on their staff.
c. The most effective teachers are attracted to the schools whose leaders have hired the best teachers.
d. The most effective school leaders are better at identifying excellent and average teachers than poorer ones.

66. Which of the following actions best illustrates how a school leader engages with the community in a proactive manner?

a. The school leader attends all local school board meetings.
b. The school leader attends the community holiday parade.
c. The school leader hosts an award ceremony for students at the school.
d. The school leader purchases advertisement space in the local community newspaper.

67. Which of the following would be most likely to cause an administrator to look for outside resources in assisting students and their families?

a. A student is having difficulty in math class.
b. Two students participated in a physical altercation.
c. A student and his or her family are struggling financially and are in need of food and clothing.
d. A student will be the first in the family to graduate high school.

68. An elementary school conducted a pilot of a reading program over the summer and the principal must decide whether to purchase the program for implementation during the regular school year. Which of the following data points would best inform the principal's decision?

a. Feedback from the teachers who implemented the program during the summer
b. Feedback from the students who participated in the program during the summer
c. Student scores on assessments included in the reading program
d. Percentage of growth in reading performance from the beginning of the program until the conclusion of the program

69. The fine arts teacher would like to construct a mural outside of the art building. The school leader believes it is a good idea, but does not have the funds to purchase the supplies required to complete the mural. What recommendation should the school leader make to the art teacher?

a. Host a fundraiser to obtain money to purchase supplies.
b. Ask the athletic director to use money from the athletics fund.
c. Charge art students an art fee to obtain money for the mural.
d. The art teacher cannot construct the mural this school year.

70. A middle school principal decides to select and train several lead teachers in the math department to conduct action research on campus. This decision is an example of which of the following strategies?

a. Providing teachers with the opportunity to take appropriate risks for improving teaching and learning
b. Encouraging collaboration between teachers to support professional growth
c. Using data-driven decision making to improve student performance
d. Giving teachers a voice in school decisions

Constructed Response

1. A group of parents have become increasingly disruptive at basketball games at the high school where you are the principal. There has been swearing, yelling, derogatory comments, etc. from the home bleachers. In 150-300 words, discuss how this situation could escalate, causing serious problems for the school, and outline the steps you would take to prevent this from happening.

2. You are starting your first year as principal at Mendoza High School, which has a diverse student population of about 1,500 students. Over the past several years the pass rate on the state mandated English exam has been declining and is now notably lower than the pass rate in other area high schools. Last school year (prior to your beginning at the school) the English department in conjunction with the faculty audited the school's curriculum and adjusted it to align with the state standards. This year, the superintendent has told you that you will have an additional $12,000 in discretionary funds to support the initiative to increase the pass rate of the English exam. In 300-600 words, outline two important issues you should consider when preparing recommendations for the discretionary budget, explain one strategy you can use to determine budget allocations to recommend that will promote improved student performance, and explain why the strategy you have described will likely be effective.

3. You are the principal of a large suburban high school with a diverse student and teacher population. One day you overhear a group of students discussing one of their classmates and her relationship with the chemistry teacher, Mr. Bolyn. The students are debating if their classmate and Mr. Bolyn have had sexual relations yet or not. In 150-300 words, explain how you would address this situation.

Answer Key and Explanations for Test #1

Multiple Choice Questions

1. A: All the information sources are valid and useful, but a school leader must ensure that the vison and goals of the school align with school, local, state, and federal policies first. After that alignment is confirmed, other information sources can be considered to develop the school's vision and goals.

2. D: School funding comes from a variety of sources, but for most states, the primary source of school funding is local property taxes. The federal government provides some funding, but this funding is usually unsubstantial and may fluctuate due to the changing budget decisions at the federal level. The state governments also provide funding to schools based on income and/or sales taxes, and for a minority of states, state funding can be the primary source of school funding. This is true for California, Hawaii, Michigan, New Mexico, Minnesota, Kansas, and Washington. The primary source of school funding in most states, however, is property taxes within the school district. Both residences and commercial properties are taxed, and a portion of those taxes are allocated to school districts. Schools and school districts often also seek grants and donations from foundations to supplement the school's budget.

3. A: Individual students have different learning styles, skills, strengths, and weaknesses, so it is important to administer multiple and varied assessments to assemble as comprehensive a picture as possible of each student's existing knowledge, new learning, and instructional needs. Multiple assessments are not used to keep students from forgetting. Summative assessments following instruction are not sufficient as they do not continuously assess student learning and progress, and they do not enable teachers to adjust ongoing instruction to be more effective as formative assessments made during instruction do.

4. A: According to research findings, transformational school leaders model and promote staff development and self-improvement by building school structures that encourage staff members to participate in decision-making, delegating responsibilities judiciously as needed, and supporting staff when they operate autonomously. Transformational school leaders encourage teacher autonomy in decision-making, strive to attain full staff consensus rather than overriding staff in determining school priorities, and communicate these priorities to staff and students to develop a strong sense of purpose overall.

5. C: The school leader observing classroom instruction also provides opportunities to observe students in the learning process. Classroom observations can provide valuable information about instructional delivery, teacher quality, and student performance. Reviewing classroom observation data in conjunction with student academic performance data can provide the school leader with a more well-rounded understanding of the quality of learning on campus.

6. C: Cooperative learning, the process of facilitating student collaboration, develops social skills, teamwork, individual and collective responsibility, and group interdependence. The Socratic method is useful for facilitating student engagement, assessing student learning, and fostering critical thinking, but is not useful for delivering instruction. Project-based learning is useful for active, hands-on learning experiences and does not require technology to be implemented effectively. Technology is a useful tool for delivering instruction, but is not required; technology is also effective when students utilize technology to engage in the learning process, making technology more student-centered.

7. A: A supportive school climate occurs when students have resources readily available to them that can help them feel supported and to overcome challenges that they may face. The resources available should be based on student needs, such as counseling, mentorship, social activities, and others. A supportive school climate should foster peer relationships among peers intentionally rather than allowing them to happen by chance because students share common schedules. While policy handbooks for students are useful, they do not directly contribute to a supportive school environment. On the other hand, student interactions with adults on campus can directly impact students' feelings of being supported.

8. C: The campus technology plan will include information such as when the computers were purchased, how they should be maintained, and when the computers should be replaced. If it is time to replace the computers, the school leader needs to identify what funds in the budget can be used to purchase new computers. If it is not time to replace the computers, the school leader may request technical support for improving the functionality of the computers.

9. C: Staff growth though professional development is important. When identifying professional development for staff members, school leaders should consider school goals as well as individual goals of staff members. This will ensure that staff members are equipped to contribute to achieving school goals but also grow in areas that they have established personal goals.

10. D: Professional development sessions that take place over time, in contrast to single-session trainings, are more likely to have an impact on teacher performance. Additionally, when a cohort of teachers participates in a training, there is opportunity for collaboration and collective accountability. There are benefits of providing individualized professional development opportunities for teachers. However, when these self-paced trainings are not time bound or accompanied by accountability measures, they are less likely to have a direct impact on current teacher performance.

11. A: According to the New Teacher Project (2011), design standards for effective teacher evaluation systems include evaluating teachers a minimum of once yearly, using multiple levels (4 or 5) for rating teachers, basing evaluations on clear instructional excellence standards prioritizing student learning, using multiple performance measures emphasizing teacher impact on student academic progress, making frequent observations and giving critical and/or constructive feedback, and making evaluation outcomes significant by using them as a major factor in important teacher employment decisions.

12. B: The disproportionate number of students suspended from school based on race may indicate that there are beliefs influencing how teachers relate to students. The school principal needs to identify if there is evidence of this in the school culture and whether campus policies perpetuate negative beliefs.

13. A: When a school leader attends a district school board meeting in an unfamiliar community, he or she is likely to encounter issues that were not prevalent in his previous community. If the school leader is receptive to change, he or she is likely to expand understanding of issues and grow as a school leader by experiencing a variety of perspectives. Seeing areas of disagreement (B) and seeing differences between district and school vision(D) can be helpful in addressing conflict and working to unify a school or district's vision, but is does not necessarily help develop the school leader's perspectives. Learning to run school board meetings (C) does not help with developing beliefs about educational issues.

14. A: When a school leader has clearly and effectively communicated the school vision and goals, others will be able to describe them in their own words. They will be able to communicate the vision and goals to others and explain the rationale behind them. Stakeholders who understand the vision and goals will propose ideas and actions that are aligned to the vision and will understand how they can participate in or contribute to achieving the vision.

15. D: In a cycle of continuous school improvement driven by data that they collect and analyze, schools and leaders should first conduct a needs assessment for their school to identify where to focus improvement efforts. Once they have identified needs, they should set specific improvement goals. Then they should reflect on their teaching and leading practices for further informing improvement. This enables implementing improvement strategies. Another necessary step is to assess progress during and following implementation.

16. A: By attending district school board meetings, a school leader new to a school and community can get a good idea of how diverse the school district and city or county; witness how school boards unite and organize diverse schools, giving them a common framework (B); see how schools can differ widely whether they are far apart or close together (C); and realize how managing an entire school district differs from managing a single school (D), promoting new insight and respect for school boards.

17. B: The NSBA acknowledges that school districts ARE committed to giving students healthy nutrition. However, it also points out that many school districts, already underfunded, cannot afford the additional expense of meeting the law's stricter nutrition standards as written—particularly because many of its regulations are not funded. Students are going hungry not because the regulations limit food amounts, but because they dislike the food, do not eat it, and so it goes wasted.

18. D: Letters and automated calls are acceptable forms of communication, but communication is most effective when parents and community members have the opportunity to engage in two-way conversation. Hosting a meeting gives participants a chance to ask questions and provide feedback to school leadership.

19. C: The DOJ collaborated with the ED in producing a positive school discipline guidance package as part of the SSDI to prevent or reduce student movement from schools to justice and correctional systems, not match school discipline to practices in those systems; replace disciplinary exclusion with better alternatives, rather than regard student justice involvement as inevitable and wait to address that; ensure Titles IV and VI of the Civil Rights Act prohibiting discrimination are enforced, which is the DOJ's job; and establish fair disciplinary practices to keep all students in school, not exclude any.

20. B: Ways that school leaders have appropriately involved students in school improvement efforts include allowing students to plan school-wide forums (A), conduct school-wide surveys (B), participate in hiring school leaders (C), and testify before education committees in their state legislatures, which is legal (D).

21. B: Goal progress should be communicated effectively and in a timely manner, especially to those who are instrumental in achieving the goal. The school leader should communicate progress toward a goal, whether positive or negative. When there is regression in progress or a lack of progress, two-way communication should occur with appropriate stakeholders to determine what unexpected barriers and challenges to accomplishing the goal need to be addressed. Communicating regression in progress toward a goal is necessary so that corrections can be made.

22. A: The school provides education and training to students that will make them employable in the community workforce. As a result, the school can supplement or adjust school programming to respond to the needs of the community, such as training students in particular employment fields that are experiencing a shortage within the community. Many schools, especially secondary schools, partner with their local community colleges and community organizations to identify employment trends in order to support the local community and increase the likelihood that graduates can obtain employment.

23. C: A successful new teacher induction program will provide opportunities for new teachers to collaborate with one another and with more experienced teachers. Additionally, a successful program will incorporate leadership development opportunities for new teachers to explore and refine their leadership skills. New teachers should receive strategic professional coaching and be assigned a mentor based on experience and effectiveness of the mentoring staff member. While the school leader is responsible for ensuring that an effective induction program in place, there are other instructional staff and campus leaders who can add value to the induction program by facilitating various aspects of the program.

24. A: The best strategy the principal can use to establish a continuous improvement cycle is to assess students at regular intervals and adjust instruction based on the data. Benchmark exams are typically shorter assessments over selected objectives rather than large comprehensive assessments. Data from these assessments reflect the mastery of objectives that are recently taught and are aligned to the pacing of the curriculum scope and sequence. Testing in less frequent intervals can also be helpful if the data is used to adjust instruction immediately rather than informing plans for the subsequent school year.

25. D: The online literacy program collects valuable data, but the data must be accessible by instructional decision makers for them to be able to make data-driven instructional decisions. Collecting data without being able to access it is not effective for data-driven decision making. In order for data to be useful, it must be easily accessible by those who need it in a timely manner. In this scenario, teachers and administrators would be able to access all the data in one location, which would facilitate using that data to make decisions using that data.

26. B: Experts believe that every school leader is motivated to conduct good teacher evaluations. However, they find one of the most important factors is whether school leaders make time to observe teachers regularly and frequently, even if only briefly each time. They emphasize that school leaders must evaluate teachers in a continuous process rather than a series of isolated events.

27. B: Despite the students not showing growth on the district benchmark test, there is no evidence of the program's efficacy or inefficacy. First, the time period may be too short to determine if the program is effective. Secondly, it is unknown if the program was intended to have a direct impact on student performance measured by the benchmark exam. To determine the program's efficacy going forward, the leadership team must develop a plan for data collection and analysis at regular intervals. Only then can the leadership team determine the programs efficacy and whether the program should continue to be implemented on campus.

28. C: Diverse students are frequently overrepresented in special education due to inadequate educator knowledge and/or preparation for distinguishing such differences vs. true disabilities affecting learning and performance. School leaders address this inequity best by analyzing assessment instruments used to evaluate students for special education—which often require accommodations, modifications, or replacement with alternative assessments for diverse learners—rather than grade-level placement procedures because these students need instruction enabling them to perform at grade level, special education teaching strategies, or special curriculum and expectations, all of which are after the fact.

29. D: School system guidelines recommend that, in giving teachers observational feedback, school leaders should focus feedback discussions by developing open-ended questions that target specific areas for each teacher, explicitly name two or three teacher strengths they observed, identify one area for improvement that will make the most impact on student learning and teacher development, and develop a few specific and attainable next steps for each teacher to take. Effective observational feedback should include strengths and weaknesses and recommendations for next steps should be clear and attainable.

30. C: Evaluating and revising campus-based assessments to ensure alignment to standards demonstrates a commitment to school-wide rigorous instruction. Assessments should accurately measure the standards. Increasing the offering of advanced placement and dual credit courses supports rigorous curriculum for some students who qualify, but does not impact rigor school wide. Similarly, increasing participation in college entrance exams does not raise the rigor of instruction on campus, but encourages students to seek and prepare for college admittance.

31. B: The principal should determine which professional development sessions that teachers are attending and whether those sessions are aligned to the curriculum, instruction, and programs on campus. The professional development sessions may be informative but may not be practically applicable to the campus if they are not aligned with campus goals. For example, if a teacher attends a professional development session on project-based learning, yet the campus does not implement nor support project-based learning, there will be little to no evidence of changes in instructional practice on campus as a result of attendance to that session.

32. A: The process of continuous improvement is the ongoing act of assessing performance and adjusting efforts in order to improve that performance. In order to implement a process of continuous improvement, there must be procedures of evaluation developed and implemented at regular checkpoints. Based on these regular evaluations, the leadership team can identify areas of improvement and initiate interventions and actions based on those identified areas. In schools, the regular evaluation of progress toward the campus vision and goals can be developed into a process of continuous improvement. However, campus leaders must focus on both the strengths and weaknesses of the campus in this process. Deficient areas can be improved to perform to standard, while areas performing at standard can be innovated for improvement.

33. C: Researchers have identified a number of transformational school leader practices promoting organizational staff learning, and the most effective transformational leaders best promote organizational learning by modeling ongoing learning in their own practices and affording staff opportunities to learn from peers. Demonstrating their high expectations for both students and teachers is important, but not necessarily central to organizational learning. While researching effective instructional practices and training staff on implementation is also useful, this approach is less aligned with transformational leadership.

34. C: Community business owners and employees are included among stakeholders in education; however, the school leader is less likely to survey them than those more key to this particular topic, including the superintendent of schools, administrators in the central office (A), members of the local school board, parents of the students (B), the students themselves, the teachers, and the paraprofessionals working at the school (D).

35. C: School principals should look for evidence of learning when conducting a classroom observation. Students should be given opportunities to respond and demonstrate learning throughout the lesson so that the teacher and the observer can determine whether students are learning the content. These opportunities may occur as questioning strategies, discussion, or through guided and independent practice. It is important for teachers to be comfortable with the instructional content and method of delivery, but this is not a primary focus of a classroom observation as a novice teacher can be nervous yet still effective. Additionally, the physical classroom setup should be conducive to learning but is not the primary focus of a classroom observation.

36. D: Effective new teacher induction programs should focus on supporting not only the new teachers, but also the school leaders who guide them. This requires offering professional development not only to new teachers, but equally to their mentors, school leaders, and other site leaders. Effective induction programs use research-based and standards-based assessment instruments to assess and inform new teacher performance. The ultimate goal of teacher induction programs that make teachers more effective is to improve student achievement.

37. A: A school leader must develop a plan for assessing and monitoring progress toward established goals. When monitoring is done consistently, the school leader will be aware of whether the school is meeting, exceeding, or falling short of established goals in a timely manner. Regularly monitoring progress toward goals will allow the school leader opportunity to make corrections in the strategies and implement actions, if needed.

38. B: Reading and writing skills are best taught and reinforced within the context of subject matter content. Creating a cross-curricular focus on reading and writing skills would best address the gap in performance among students who are not reading at grade level. Increasing opportunities for students to read is beneficial, but is less effective in closing opportunity gaps, especially when opportunities to engage in reading are voluntary such as after school or at home. Targeted test preparation has limited efficacy if attendance is voluntary and student performance is not monitored.

39. D: According to the National Center for Education Statistics (NCES), school leaders should *not* ignore the political environment because political support and connections can greatly benefit obtaining funding and legislation. They should avoid overly technical language with most stakeholder audiences who will not understand industry jargon. Leaders should communicate with stakeholders in sensitive situations. However, leaders should avoid engaging in large-scale open forums which can obstruct progress by being unfocused, unstructured, and may admit too many voices.

40. D: A school leader cannot use their professional influence or position to solicit votes for a candidate on campus. Public school educators have a right to engage in the political process outside of school, but these activities cannot interfere with their job duties or cause a conflict of interest.

41. B: School improvement plans have been found to increase parental meeting and student school attendance; student enrollment and achievement; parental involvement in policies, procedures, advocacy, organizing, and events; and to decrease student behavior problems while increasing student achievement. School system leaders have also established central office policies and structures that increased parental engagement, not only in individual schools but also system-wide.

42. C: According to the Collaborative for Academic, Social, and Emotional Learning (CASEL), effective SEL programs incorporate sequenced and systematic programming across all grade levels, monitor the programming continuously, offer opportunities for students to practice the skills they learn, and coordinate school environments with community environments.

43. C: It is important to involve stakeholders in the development of the school vision to help incorporate their varied perspectives into the vision and to increase buy in for the vision. Without buy in, community members and stakeholders may oppose the school vision and withdraw their support and resources for the school and school leadership.

44. C: An integrated management system unites all digital management systems into one total structure, facilitating shared objectives and working as a unit to achieve them. According to experts, a school not using any digital management system is not the best candidate without experience or systems to integrate. A school using one system and not planning more does not need integration. The ideal school uses one or more systems and plans adding more. Systems within an integrated management system share policies, documentation, processes, and procedures; a school wanting these separated does not want integration.

45. A: No Child Left Behind's stress on accountability has shifted school counselors' responsibilities away from mental health (MH) toward academic performance, reducing professional support services and resulting in limited resources. Students are routinely diagnosed with serious disorders and prescribed costly treatments, despite the fact that prevention and MH promotion can address most issues (B), is representative of inadequate research. The claim that MH resources are not proportionate or equitable (C) represents uneven resource distribution. That cultural traditions marginalize school MH priority (D) represents stigmatizing MH issues.

46. A: Calibration is the process of exploring and reaching consensus about learning standards, goals, and definitions at building, system-wide, and district-wide levels. Student data focus (B) yields in-depth information, for example, how well students are meeting specific, time-limited learning objectives. Educator engagement (C) alleviates faculty mistrust under external accountability pressures and facilitates systemic, sustainable change. Supportive technology (D) facilitates teacher access to data and shares reciprocal support with data team collaboration.

47. B: Professional Learning Committees (PLC) are designed to facilitate collaboration among teachers based on grade levels, subject area, or other commonalities. In PLCs, educators use quantitative and qualitative data to make decisions about students and are guided by the following questions: What do we want students to learn? What do we do if they do not learn it? What do we do if they learn it? Communicating with parents and submitting reports often include sharing of data, but do not necessarily indicate that the data is used to make decisions. Requiring teachers to host tutorial sessions for students is a beneficial intervention, but may not be a directive based on data.

48. B: Although a technology budget cut is bad news, the principal would want to assess the current technology equipment on campus first. If the campus is already technology rich, the budget cut may not result in a drastic impact to instruction for the upcoming school year and little to no action may be necessary. After assessing the current technology equipment on campus, the principal can determine if the equipment meets the needs for the upcoming school year and, if not, how to make adjustments.

49. D: Attending a mandated training session indicates that the leader failed to identify that the training was needed for themselves, but instead needed to be directed by someone else to attend. Self-reflection involves reflecting on one's own performance in comparison to a set of leadership expectations and standards.

50. B: The school leader can form a parent focus group in order to gather feedback and opinions on decisions to be made at the school. A focus group would allow multiple parents to participate and would foster two-way communication. Two-way communication allows both parties to participate and contribute. One-way communication methods can gather input from others or deliver information, but they do not allow stakeholders to actively participate in the decision-making process.

51. A: The Supportive School Discipline Initiative (SSDI) included guidance for positive school discipline practices to keep students in school by providing alternatives to exclusionary methods like suspension and expulsion. This guidance was produced jointly by the US Departments of Education and Justice to ensure enforcement of federal civil rights protections against discrimination. It provides school resources with helpful information rather than getting it from them. The SSDI's purpose was to keep student discipline from escalating to the police or prison systems, not to continue this trend.

52. A: Data showing school improvement goals that are behind schedule indicate a need to update the school improvement plan—either by adjusting completion time criteria if school leaders and staff determine they were unrealistic in either case, or by adjusting instruction to be more effective if they determine current methods are delaying progress.

53. B: Student trust in the teacher and interest in the class lead to success versus mistrust and disinterest (A). Ambition in learning leads to success versus ambivalence toward learning (C). Industry in pursuing learning goals promotes student success versus disengagement from boredom or discouragement from difficulty (D). However, success is more likely through a balance of student autonomy and teacher control versus too much of either one (B).

54. C: Meeting with a diverse group of stakeholders from the community will give the new principal a well-rounded perspective of the community. Researching the community online, reviewing student data, and talking with staff are all effective methods of collecting information, but speaking directly with community members is a better source of more insightful information.

55. C: Utilizing community services builds partnerships and relationships between the school and the community, which can have long-range benefits for both parties. When businesses provide mentors for students, they are engaged in activities over time that can have a positive impact on the school community.

56. B: Research finds the relationship between school leadership and student outcomes is indirect rather than direct. Rather than motivating student achievement directly, effective school leadership promotes a school climate conducive to learning. Substantial research has demonstrated that there is a relationship between school leadership and student outcomes, although the relationship is indirect.

57. A: To realize instructional change over time, professional development (PD) must be provided on an ongoing basis and reinforced through repetition and classroom follow-up activities. Teachers need theoretical understanding not only of the theory underling instructional practices, but also of how they can apply theory to practice. PD is best administered as a component of a comprehensive, systematic, district-supported educational reform process. When school leaders furnish PD, they should be careful to avoid topics lacking research support, unrelated to student learning, and popular new fads.

58. C: Each of the options represents a supportive way of promoting professional development, but choice C is primarily an individual activity and not a way of building up a collaborative learning environment among professionals. Action research is the process of doing informal studies in the school environment to try to find improved practices. While the research is often done alone, the intent of action research is to share with other members of the learning community, making it a collaborative effort in most cases. Professional learning communities (PLCs) are teams of educators who work together to identify concerns and meet needs together and is an excellent way for teachers to improve their skills through professional collaboration. Structured observations are usually something the school administration takes on to ensure a quality control on teaching, but even though it often is top-down oriented, the process is inherently collaborative in that one professional comes and observes another teacher and provides specific feedback to help improve professional practices.

59. C: When scheduling parent meetings for large groups of parents, the school leader should consider the time of the day and the day of the week that these meetings are to be held. The goal of these meetings is to effectively communicate with parents in a group setting, so the school leader needs to ensure that the scheduled time and day of the meeting accommodates the majority of parents for maximum attendance.

60. A: A leader effectively monitors goal progress by implementing clear checkpoints and milestones for goal activities. Each goal should be broken down into smaller goals, or milestones, that can be reviewed at regular intervals. This allows the leader to analyze progress toward the goal on a timeline so that if there is not sufficient progress toward the goal, there is time to intervene and make changes to the action steps.

61. D: To collaborate effectively with teachers regarding assessment, school leaders must know classroom assessment principles, including that no assessment instrument is error free (A)—that is, all assessment involves some error; that authors and users of assessments typically underestimate testing error (B); that reliability, that is, getting consistent results across repeated administrations, applies to test scores and not the tests themselves (C); and that good assessment is not only valid (tests what it means or claims to test) and reliable but also ethical and fair (D).

62. A: A school leader must identify key stakeholders within the school community, including those with competing perspectives. The school leader should meet with the group of disgruntled teachers, also, to facilitate two-way communication. The school leader will have an opportunity to listen to and address the group members' concerns, while the teachers will have an opportunity to hear the rationale for certain policies and procedures.

63. A: Student placement in courses should be based on relevant data. Automatically enrolling students in advanced placement courses without reviewing data could result in students being placed in classes that are too rigorous while students who were not previously enrolled could miss an opportunity to be placed in a challenging course. School leaders should monitor student performance data, ensure rigor and alignment of curriculum, and provide campus-wide opportunities for students when possible. To provide all students with preparation for and access to a challenging curriculum, students should have opportunities for an appropriate level of rigorous instruction based on their current academic performance.

64. D: School leaders are responsible for knowing and enforcing student and parent rights to privacy and confidentiality of educational records under the Family Educational Rights and Privacy Act (FERPA) and Individuals with Disabilities Education Act (IDEA). They must know and understand exceptions to these laws, which can require them to disclose student records to law enforcement and others. School leaders are responsible for both disclosing information to third parties and obtaining the written parental consent required for such disclosures. They are also responsible for creating policy governing access to student records by parties other than parents and eligible students.

65. B: Multiple research studies find that the most effective school leaders are better at identifying the teachers best and worst at increasing student performance among their existing faculty. However, researchers cannot determine whether the fact that effective school leaders also hire the best experienced teachers is more attributable to better leader ability in choosing teachers or to excellent teachers' attraction to schools with the best existing faculty quality. Researchers do observe that school leaders cannot differentiate quality among average teachers as well as they can differentiate better from poorer teachers due to lesser contrast.

66. B: Participating in school- and district-sponsored events is not always the same as engaging with the greater community. Community stakeholders can include members of the community who do not have children enrolled in the school district but are contributors to the community as a whole. These stakeholders may include business owners, community organization leaders, and residents near the school. Additionally, community engagement involves opportunities for two-way communication between the school leader and community members. Attending the community parade gives the school leader an opportunity to represent the school at a community event and engage with community stakeholders. This increases the school leader's visibility in the community and demonstrates that the school is a part of the community that it serves.

67. C: Depending on school budget and resources, student needs that are not directly related to student safety and academic performance may not be able to be addressed using school resources. Many community resources used to support schools are targeted toward students in need. These types of resources may address physical needs of students and their families, such as providing food, clothing, toiletries, haircuts and grooming, or helping adults find jobs.

68. D: Student growth is the best data point to inform the principal as to whether the reading program was effective. An effective program would result in individual and collective student growth as measured by a pre- and post-assessment. Feedback from students and teachers is valuable and can be considered in the budgeting decision; however, a principal would not want to purchase a program if it does not produce results, even if the students and teachers viewed the program positively.

69. A: Fundraisers are a common way for schools to secure money and resources outside of school budgets. Fundraisers should always be conducted within the policies and procedures outlined by the school campus and the school district.

70. A: Supporting teachers in conducting action research on campus is an example of giving them opportunities to take risks for improving teaching and learning. Action research allows the teacher to identify the area of improvement and hypothesize which actions or strategies may lead to improving the identified area. Action research allows teachers to problem solve using solutions that they have developed which gives them the opportunity to take risks.

Constructed Response

1. Essay question graders commonly look for the following elements in a strong response: strong content knowledge, clear organization, and effective arguments or examples. Language and usage are not usually strictly graded, but can make a big impact on the clarity of your ideas.

Please use the provided rubric to make sure your response meets these common criteria. Try to have a friend or family member grade your response for you or take a break after writing your response and return to grade it with fresh eyes.

CONSTRUCTED RESPONSE RUBRIC

Domain	Description
Content Knowledge	• The response directly addresses every part of the prompt. • The response demonstrates independent knowledge of the topic. • The response discusses the topic at an appropriate depth.
Organization	• The response introduces the topic, usually with a thesis statement or by restating the prompt. • The response directly addresses the prompt by providing a clear and concise answer or solution. • The answer or solution is supported by logical arguments or evidence. • The response restates the main idea in the conclusion.
Arguments and Examples	• The response provides a reasonable answer to the prompt. • The answer is supported by strong reasoning or evidence. • The response develops ideas logically and connects ideas to one another. • The reasoning and evidence provided act to support a unified main idea.
Language and Usage	• The response demonstrates effective use of grammar and uses varied sentence structure throughout the response. • The response demonstrates correct use of spelling, punctuation, and capitalization. • The response demonstrates strong and varied use of vocabulary relevant to the topic and appropriate for the intended audience.

2. Essay question graders commonly look for the following elements in a strong response: strong content knowledge, clear organization, and effective arguments or examples. Language and usage are not usually strictly graded, but can make a big impact on the clarity of your ideas.

Please use the provided rubric to make sure your response meets these common criteria. Try to have a friend or family member grade your response for you or take a break after writing your response and return to grade it with fresh eyes.

Constructed Response Rubric

Domain	Description
Content Knowledge	• The response directly addresses every part of the prompt. • The response demonstrates independent knowledge of the topic. • The response discusses the topic at an appropriate depth.
Organization	• The response introduces the topic, usually with a thesis statement or by restating the prompt. • The response directly addresses the prompt by providing a clear and concise answer or solution. • The answer or solution is supported by logical arguments or evidence. • The response restates the main idea in the conclusion.
Arguments and Examples	• The response provides a reasonable answer to the prompt. • The answer is supported by strong reasoning or evidence. • The response develops ideas logically and connects ideas to one another. • The reasoning and evidence provided act to support a unified main idea.
Language and Usage	• The response demonstrates effective use of grammar and uses varied sentence structure throughout the response. • The response demonstrates correct use of spelling, punctuation, and capitalization. • The response demonstrates strong and varied use of vocabulary relevant to the topic and appropriate for the intended audience.

3. Essay question graders commonly look for the following elements in a strong response: strong content knowledge, clear organization, and effective arguments or examples. Language and usage are not usually strictly graded, but can make a big impact on the clarity of your ideas.

Please use the provided rubric to make sure your response meets these common criteria. Try to have a friend or family member grade your response for you or take a break after writing your response and return to grade it with fresh eyes.

Constructed Response Rubric

Domain	Description
Content Knowledge	• The response directly addresses every part of the prompt. • The response demonstrates independent knowledge of the topic. • The response discusses the topic at an appropriate depth.
Organization	• The response introduces the topic, usually with a thesis statement or by restating the prompt. • The response directly addresses the prompt by providing a clear and concise answer or solution. • The answer or solution is supported by logical arguments or evidence. • The response restates the main idea in the conclusion.
Arguments and Examples	• The response provides a reasonable answer to the prompt. • The answer is supported by strong reasoning or evidence. • The response develops ideas logically and connects ideas to one another. • The reasoning and evidence provided act to support a unified main idea.
Language and Usage	• The response demonstrates effective use of grammar and uses varied sentence structure throughout the response. • The response demonstrates correct use of spelling, punctuation, and capitalization. • The response demonstrates strong and varied use of vocabulary relevant to the topic and appropriate for the intended audience.

Practice Test #2

Multiple Choice Questions

1. The PTO president expressed concern to the school principal about the recent announcement to purchase new science curriculum for ninth and tenth-grade students. He expressed that there was a greater need for college preparation materials for students. Which of the following responses from the principal is best?

a. Purchasing science curriculum was the economic choice because it will benefit a greater number of students for a smaller cost.
b. College preparation materials will be considered for purchase for the upcoming school year.
c. Student performance data demonstrates that students are already performing at a satisfactory level on college entrance exams.
d. One of the school goals for the year is to improve student performance in science and the curriculum purchase supports that goal.

2. As school leader responsibilities have increased, distributing leadership has become more important. Distributive leadership can have additive or holistic forms. Which of the following is correct regarding these forms?

a. In the additive form, collective work by all leaders adds up to more than the sum of its parts.
b. In the holistic form, every organizational member is a leader, regardless of his or her interactions.
c. In the additive form, all organizational leaders must "sink or swim" together, not separately.
d. In the holistic form, interdependent leadership among organization members is emphasized.

3. What correctly represents National Education Association (NEA) guidelines for school acceptable use policies (AUPs) regarding classroom Internet technology?

a. It should have a policy statement including covered computer services and student use conditions.
b. It should have a definition section covering important terms used, but a preamble is not necessary.
c. It should include a section that defines acceptable use, but not one that defines unacceptable use.
d. It should include a violations or sanctions section, which should only define violations of the policy.

4. Which of the following would be the most effective way to engage parents in student behavior management systems?

a. Distribute the behavioral code of conduct to parents at the beginning of the school year.
b. Find parent volunteers to help enforce the behavioral code of conduct.
c. Ask for feedback from parents on the draft of the behavioral code of conduct before it is finalized.
d. Develop a behavioral code of conduct in partnership with teachers, parents, and students.

5. Which of the following is the best example of differentiated instruction based on product?

a. Teach different content for different students.
b. Allow students to choose between writing an essay or recording a video for an assignment.
c. Give students different version of assessments.
d. Assign some students to watch a video while others read an article.

6. Surveyed school principals have reported that which of the following has been adversely affected since standards-based accountability systems were implemented?

a. Teacher morale
b. Curriculum and instruction
c. Student assessment practices
d. Expectations and achievement

7. Researchers have identified which of the following practices that successful education leaders recommend to advocate for educational excellence and equity?

a. They develop equity skills that spread through the learning community.
b. They study system inequities to discover solutions to the problems.
c. They study equitable leadership to discover their parts in the problems.
d. They advise others to develop collaborative approaches across systems.

8. Which of these is a valid guideline for school leaders to support staff throughout their professional development (PD)?

a. To be job-embedded and school-based, PD must occur in the school building.
b. For effective PD, teachers must not learn passively, but be actively involved.
c. Because teachers are the ones involved in PD, it should be teacher-centered.
d. PD must be done independently to ensure individual learning and growth.

9. Nationally, public-school districts receive the largest proportion of funding from which of the following sources?

a. Federal government
b. Their city government
c. The state government
d. Various other sources

10. Which of the following is true regarding information and data that teachers should consider when planning for differentiated instruction?

a. Special population identification and past academic performance are the only data that teachers should consider when planning for differentiated instruction.
b. Formative assessment is not useful when planning for differentiated instruction.
c. Student interests should be a major determining factor when planning for differentiated instruction.
d. Student performance data, interests, and learning styles should all be considered when planning for differentiated instruction.

11. How can a school leader evaluate and improve the school curriculum for cultural and racial equity?

a. Instruct teachers to view curriculum as pluralistic and unchanging.
b. Include multicultural education within the school curriculum goals.
c. Assure books include diversity but not look for prejudiced content.
d. Focus multicultural education on foods, festivals, and fun activities.

12. A math intervention program that was implemented on a high school campus for the previous school year was funded by a grant that is expired. The principal must determine whether to fund the program using the local budget or to eliminate the program. Which of the following data points would best inform the principal as to whether the math intervention program should continue to be funded?

a. Student attendance in the program
b. Feedback from students regarding the program
c. Student math performance data from the beginning of the school year compared to the end of the school year
d. Student performance on the state mandated assessment for the previous school year

13. Which of the following strategies is least likely to improve teacher practice?

a. Conducting regular classroom observations and providing written feedback to teachers
b. Pairing novice teachers with an experienced teacher for peer coaching
c. Providing teachers with aggregated student performance data each grading cycle
d. Facilitating professional learning communities for teacher collaboration by grade level and by content area

14. Which of the following is not accurate regarding school leaders' engagement of faculty and staff in ongoing self-assessment and improvement?

a. To encourage self-direction in improving, leaders should model self-assessment and improvement.
b. To encourage self-direction in improving, leaders should actively engage workers.
c. To encourage self-direction in improving, leaders should make learning accessible.
d. To encourage self-direction in improving, leaders should leave self-improvement up to employees.

15. Which of the following statements is not accurate about requirements for integrating technology comprehensively into instruction to support school vision?

a. Successful school-wide implementation of educational technology is dependent on the technology selected, not school leadership.
b. Regardless of the technology capabilities of school staff, training and professional development are needed to successfully implement educational technology school-wide.
c. School structure and organization impact the success of adopting educational technology.
d. Schools must have the resources and support for implementing technology school-wide.

16. Which of the following is true regarding how school leaders can foster equitable and inclusive educational practices?

a. The development of curriculum should solely be based on developmental appropriateness.
b. School leaders should model respect for diversity and offer multiple means for celebrating it.
c. Involving culturally diverse community stakeholders in school decisions is the responsibility of the school district.
d. Only school leaders are accountable to ensure equity for every student in all school programs.

17. Which of the following strategies would be most effective for communicating with stakeholders who speak a different language?

a. Hire translators and provide translation machines at community events.
b. Hire a bilingual principal.
c. Translate all written communications.
d. Ask students to translate for their parents.

18. Who typically makes student enrollment projections for determining school budgets?

a. District Offices of Achievement and Accountability alone project the student enrollments
b. District Offices of Achievement and Accountability with school leader revision as needed
c. The school leader alone projects the student enrollments for his or her school every year
d. Final projections are by committees from the district finance and student support offices

19. Which statement is MOST accurate concerning how school leaders can ensure that faculty instructional practices treat minority students equitably?

a. Leaders can best get teachers to model appreciation of diversity for students by talking about it.
b. If teaching practices conflict with student cultures, leaders instruct teachers to be aware of this.
c. Having all teachers know a few words or phrases in each student's L1 is simply token lip service.
d. Leaders should make sure that all staff members learn to pronounce students' names correctly.

20. Which of the following strategies for implementing technology is most closely related to leadership in implementing a school improvement plan?

a. Utilizing technology as a tool to facilitate collaboration among staff
b. Utilizing technology as a tool to administer assessments to students
c. Utilizing technology as a tool for communication among stakeholders
d. Utilizing technology as a tool to collect, organize, and analyze data for school improvement and progress monitoring

21. Which of the following is true about proactive strategies that successful school leaders have used to overcome resistance to change by school staff, families, communities, and school districts?

a. People fear change irrespective of school leader commitment.
b. Administrative support networks enhance change acceptance.
c. Establishing priorities tends to strengthen resistance to change.
d. How school leaders communicate has no impact on resistance.

22. Advanced technology integration in schools includes empowering students to engage in the learning process using technology. Which of the following best exemplifies students creating content using digital media?

a. Students access wiki pages to review lesson materials.
b. Students record themselves reading aloud for reading assessment.
c. Students design elaborate digital storybooks to prepare for a state writing exam.
d. Students create PowerPoint presentations about insects using photos from the Internet.

23. Which kind of data best helps teachers to identify strengths and needs in their teaching practices, support capacity-building, and identify specific remedial student groups?

a. Formative data
b. Summative data
c. Student profiles
d. Enrollment data

24. Of the following, which is an advantage of developing a school vision collaboratively?

a. Visions developed through collaboration can be implemented far faster.
b. Visions are clearer and more coherent when developed by collaboration.
c. Visions take longer times in the process of development, slowing change.
d. Visions tend to be more appropriate to their local school district contexts.

25. Several teachers on campus have expressed concerns to the principal that there is too much focus on standardized assessment. The teachers suggest that they develop authentic assessments for student learning. Which of the following is the best example of authentic summative assessment?

a. Benchmark tests
b. Student choice of completing a project, essay, or performance
c. Oral exams
d. Allowing students to complete homework assignments at their own pace

26. Which of the following accurately reflects evaluative criteria that school leaders should consider first when deciding to utilize community resources to support student learning?

a. Congruence with the school's vision and mission
b. Immediate impact on student achievement
c. Results from prior implementation
d. The relationship of the person or organization to the school

27. Which of the following criteria would best help a school leader to determine if the school vision and goals are appropriate?

a. The vision and goals address the areas of deficit determined by analysis of multiple sources of data.
b. The vision and goals are approved by community stakeholders.
c. The vision and goals reflect a balance of the school's strengths and weaknesses.
d. The vision and goals mirror those established by schools with similar performance history and student demographics.

28. Regarding strategies that principals can use to give teachers effective feedback, which is true?

a. Principals will make feedback fresher for teachers by delivering it unexpectedly.
b. Principals should give feedback unrelated to their expectations or teacher goals.
c. Principals enable perspective by delaying feedback after classroom observation.
d. Principals convey criticism best following strengths and by requesting solutions.

29. The school participates in a health education program that provides sex education and contraceptives to middle school students. A teacher is opposed to this program and becomes very vocal in the community about the dangers of having this program on campus. The principal begins to receive numerous phone calls and emails about the program. Which of the following actions would best help the principal refocus attention to vision and goals?

a. Issue a public statement regarding the value of health education and the alignment of the program with the school's vision.
b. Meet with the teacher who is opposed to the program to reach an agreement.
c. Ignore the phone calls and emails.
d. Hold a community meeting to discuss the program with stakeholders.

30. Which of the following is the best way to identify strategies for facilitating change?

a. Host student and teacher focus groups to solicit suggestions and ideas.
b. Conduct pilot programs and collect data to determine efficacy.
c. Study research-based and proven best practices.
d. Meet with community stakeholders to solicit suggestions and ideas.

31. How should school leaders and others analyze school data to inform the school vision?

a. Across grade levels instead of across school years
b. By subject matter rather than by student cohorts
c. By formative and summative assessment findings
d. By teachers within grades instead of across levels

32. What is the primary reason that curriculum and instruction must be aligned to assessments?

a. School leaders must be able to justify why they select curriculum and resources.
b. Teachers must know what to teach in the classroom.
c. Assessments that are not aligned with curriculum and instruction will not accurately measure what students learned.
d. Alignment of curriculum and assessments makes it easier to analyze and compare student performance data.

33. Which of the following is the most crucial question to consider when developing school goals?

a. Are the school goals based on accurate data?
b. Are the school goals achievable?
c. Are the school goals aligned with the school vision?
d. Were stakeholders given the opportunity to participate in the development of the school goals?

Refer to the following for question 34:

The school principal reviews classroom observation and feedback with assistant principals weekly but often has very few classroom observations of their own conducted in preparation for the weekly meeting. This week, a teacher complained to the principal that the feedback from their most recent evaluation was not fair because it did not provide a well-rounded view of their performance.

34. Which of the following is the best action that the principal can take to address this teacher's concern?

a. Conduct additional observations of the teacher at various days of the week, times of the day, and in varied circumstances.
b. Explain why the evaluation was accurate.
c. Find other staff members who can confirm what was written in the teacher's evaluation.
d. Show the teacher that all protocols and policies were followed in conducting the evaluation.

35. Research shows that school leaders' time spent on which of these does not predict better student achievement?

a. Making evaluations
b. Class walkthroughs
c. Coaching teachers
d. Program development

36. A school leader has decided to hire an instructional coach to support the teachers' growth. Which of the following is the most likely result of this decision?

a. The instructional coach will help the leadership team supervise and evaluate teachers.
b. The instructional coach will make the decisions regarding professional development and training on campus.
c. Having an instructional coach will eliminate the need for professional development and training on campus.
d. The instructional coach will provide individualized support to teachers to help them grow.

37. Which of the following is a practice of a school leader that facilitates family involvement in education?

a. Hiring parent facilitators using state Title I and Smart Start funds.
b. Working extended hours on campus.
c. Collaborating with parents who are already involved in school activities.
d. Sending an e-newsletter to parents weekly.

38. The National Association of Secondary School Principals (NASSP) recommendations for ethical behaviors by school leaders include the following:

I. Fulfilling their professional duties honestly and with integrity
II. Obeying all the federal, state, and local laws and regulations
III. Basing all decisions on the value of student success and well-being
IV. Acting to change laws, policies, and regulations against education goals
V. Implementing the local board of education regulations and policies

Which combination of these could MOST present a conflict for a school leader in some instances?

a. I and III
b. II and IV
c. II, IV, and V
d. III, IV, and V

39. The campus technology coordinator recommends to the principal that new desktop computers be purchased for three of the campus's computer labs. The dean of instruction recommends that classroom technology should be upgraded first. Which of the following strategies should the principal implement first to decide how to prioritize these recommendations in the school's technology budget?

a. The principal should physically inspect the current equipment to determine which is in the most need of replacement.
b. The principal should refer to the campus improvement plan to determine how the recommendations align with the vision and goals for the school.
c. The principal should seek donations from stakeholders to assist with improving technology across the campus.
d. The principal should determine which of the recommendations is most economical.

40. Which of the following statements is most accurate about why schools must collaborate with their communities in providing mental health services to remove learning barriers and improve student outcomes?

a. In many communities and states, schools are often children's only mental health service providers.
b. Due to stigma associated with mental health needs, parents avoid familiar school settings and staff.
c. According to research study findings, students are less likely to seek counseling services in schools.
d. Mental health services in schools should be separated from mental health services in communities.

41. Which of the following describes the school district policy to allow principals autonomy to spend their campus budget as they see fit?

a. Local school management
b. Hybrid financial decision-making
c. Budgetary autonomy
d. Decentralization

42. What best reflects research findings about factors influencing school achievement gaps?

a. School curriculum and resources correlate with student achievement more strongly than socioeconomic status (SES).
b. SES correlates more strongly with achievement than school resources.
c. Student SES correlates more strongly with student achievement than school curriculum does.
d. Student achievement correlates more strongly with SES and school resources than curriculum.

43. Which of the following is a primary benefit of professional learning communities?

a. They provide opportunities for teachers to share ideas.
b. They provide constructive feedback on student performance.
c. They identify areas in the curriculum that need revision.
d. They ensure that the standards-based curriculum is delivered.

44. In school-wide positive behavior support (SPBS) programs, which of the following is a procedure associated with tier 3?

a. Socio-emotional groups
b. Daily check-in and check-out
c. Intervention family support
d. Individualized interventions

45. The sixth-grade math department meets as a professional learning community and determines that overall students in sixth-grade are not performing well on the same three math objectives. However, these same students are performing satisfactorily on other math objectives. Which of the following is the most likely reason that the sixth-grade students are not mastering the identified math objectives?

a. The math teachers are ineffective in teaching the identified math objectives.
b. The curriculum is not properly aligned to address the identified math objectives.
c. The students need additional tutoring to master the identified math objectives.
d. The assessment used to measure student performance was biased.

46. Which of the following accurately describes cognitive and affective processes involved in school organizational learning and staff development?

a. Conversation and affirmation are cognitive; reflection and invitation are affective
b. Reflection and conversation are cognitive; affirmation and invitation are affective
c. Reflection and affirmation are cognitive; conversation and invitation are affective
d. Affirmation and invitation are cognitive; reflection and conversation are affective

47. Which of the following strategies would most likely encourage stakeholders to support and implement the school vision and goals?

a. Announcing the school vision and goals at a community meeting.
b. Publishing the school vision and goals on the school website.
c. Including internal and external community members in the development of the vision and goals.
d. Selecting representatives from the staff and community to be advocates for the school's vision and goals.

48. A high school principal has created instructional teams comprised of teachers from each core content area and fine arts. These teams plan instruction together and incorporate concepts from the various subjects in each of their classrooms. This strategy is an example of what type of instruction?

a. Differentiated instruction
b. Rigorous instruction
c. Cross-curricular instruction
d. Professional learning communities

49. Some successful school leaders have obtained public and financial support for their schools by communicating with community members. Which example of this is most applicable?

a. Sharing real estate data with the business community is unrelated to school success.
b. Local families are drawn to schools more by physical changes than better test scores.
c. Significant improvements for minority students are best shared within the first year.
d. Leaders should share substantial, overall school academic gains with families yearly.

50. When selecting professional development for staff, which of the following should a leader consider first?

a. The cost of the professional development
b. Whether the professional development has been effective on other campuses
c. The areas of deficit of staff based on observations and evaluations
d. The alignment of the professional development with the campus vision and goals

51. A school leader and the leadership team have begun developing a plan for implementing the school goals. The leader has identified the necessary action steps, the persons responsible for each step, and the time frames in which each step should be taken. Which of the following is the most appropriate next step for finalizing the plan?

a. Identify the resources needed for each step and evidence of implementation.
b. Share the plan with persons who will be responsible for completing an action step.
c. Present the plan to staff.
d. Plan future meetings with staff to monitor progress in implementing the plan.

52. School emergency response team organization is modeled after the Incident Command System (ICS) of Homeland Security's National Incident Management System (NIMS). Main ICS functions include Finance. Which of the ICS Management Systems identifies services and resources to support incident response needs?

a. Logistics
b. Planning
c. Command
d. Operations

53. Which of the following is the best example of summative assessment?

a. Standardized tests
b. Homework assignments
c. Practice assignments completed in class
d. Projects

54. Which of the following best represents a threat to an emotionally safe campus environment?

a. Bullying
b. Crowded classrooms
c. High teacher turnover
d. High rates of student suspensions

55. A school principal reflects on their personal performance during the most recent school year. Based on data and their own reflection, the principal noticed that many of the plans that were created at the beginning of the school year were not implemented properly because he or she was not able to get all of the action items done. Which of the following action plans might help the principal improve time management in the future?

a. Use data to make more effective decisions.
b. Prioritize activities that are most directly related to the campus vision and goals.
c. Hold members of the leadership team accountable for their task completion.
d. Increase the number of hours that he or she spends on campus.

Refer to the following for question 56:

A new school principal administered a survey to school staff to assess the perceived culture of the school. The data from the survey showed that most of the staff felt that all ideas for the school came from the top and were forced down. The school principal wants to shift the culture and encourage staff to be innovative.

56. Which of the following strategies would best help the principal to meet this goal?

a. Create action committees made up of teachers and staff and give the committees time and resources to generate solutions to campus needs.
b. Place a suggestion box in the teachers' lounge and encourage teachers to submit their ideas for consideration.
c. Inform the staff that there are positions on the Shared Decision-Making Committee for teachers and that they would feel more represented if they engaged in the process.
d. Host a town hall meeting and allow participants to share their ideas publicly.

57. What must school leaders consider to mobilize and develop community school support?

a. Businesses and community-based organizations use the same language that educators use.
b. Exchanging and matching visions, missions, wants, and needs with stakeholders is sufficient.
c. Prospective community partners primarily want to know how collaboration benefits schools.
d. Prospective partner motivations are as varied as the organizations interested in partnership.

58. What is the primary purpose of professional learning communities?

a. To hold teachers accountable
b. To make it easier to monitor teaching and learning
c. To facilitate collaboration among teachers
d. To set and achieve instructional goals

59. The math teachers on campus suggest to the school leader that improved academic performance in math should be one of the school's goals. The school leader agrees and decides to create a measurable goal for student math performance. Which of the following is the best example of a measurable math performance goal?

a. 95% of eighth-grade students will demonstrate growth in their math class.
b. All eighth-grade students will be successful in their math class.
c. Eighth-grade students will earn at least a B average in their math class.
d. 90% of eighth-grade students will earn at least a B average in their math class.

60. Developing a school safety plan requires the participation of which of the following and for which reason?

a. School leaders and staff, because only they know their school and students best
b. School personnel only, because schools are for controlling as well as for learning
c. The entire community, because school crime data reflect community crime data
d. Law enforcement and mental health professionals, because they address crimes

61. Which of the following is true about school leaders as role models for teachers in professional development (PD)?

a. School leaders should facilitate PD activities.
b. School leaders should participate in PD with teachers.
c. School leaders should monitor teacher implementation of learning from PD sessions.
d. School leaders should determine the PD offered to teachers.

62. A high school principal determines that it is no longer financially viable to sponsor the fine arts program at the school. Enrollment in fine arts courses has steadily decreased over the past four school years and the expenses of the program have exceeded the budget. However, the principal knows that many stakeholders in the community feel strongly about having a fine arts program. Which of the following represents the best action for the school principal?

a. Continue to offer the fine arts program.
b. Make an announcement to the students and staff that there will not be a fine arts program next year.
c. Host a fundraiser for the fine arts program.
d. Host a meeting to explain to stakeholders the reasons for eliminating the fine arts program.

63. Which of the following most correctly represents criteria requiring a school to hold a Manifestation Determination Review for a student who receives special education services?

a. The school seeks a discipline-related placement change for more than 10 days in a row.
b. The school suspends a student on a one-time basis for 10 or fewer consecutive days.
c. The school suspends a student for 10 or more days in a school year for any reason.
d. The school creates or revises a behavior intervention plan.

64. The US Department of Homeland Security has adopted the National Incident Management System (NIMS) for all federal, state, and local government agencies in emergency response. This system includes the Incident Command System (ICS). School district and building emergency response teams are organized based on ICS management functions. Which of these functions develops incident response objectives?

a. Planning
b. Logistics
c. Command
d. Operations

65. A school is in the process of implementing a campus-wide adoption of new technology. Which of the following is LEAST central to the role of a school leader acting to implement this change?

a. Leading by example and using technology with teachers and students
b. Attending professional development classes and keeping current with the research
c. Establishing conditions for change by setting high learning expectations and encouraging teacher effort
d. Encouraging use of the new technology, offering teachers learning opportunities, and resolving implementation problems

66. Which of the following sources and types of data would be best to use to provide feedback to teachers so that they can improve student learning?

a. Classroom observations, student class grades, and summative assessment data
b. Formative assessment data, attendance data, and behavior data
c. Classroom observations, survey data, and diagnostic testing data
d. Formative assessment data, diagnostic testing data, and projected performance data

67. Which of the following is an appropriate example of an action that school leaders can take to change negative school cultures and employee attitudes that interfere with realizing school visions?

a. Observe indicators of school culture among students and staff.
b. Design professional development sessions for teachers that address school culture.
c. Frequently recount successful accomplishments of goals related to school vision.
d. Hold annual ceremonies for celebrating successes.

68. Which statement is true with respect to segregated educational services for individual student needs and integrated comprehensive educational services?

a. Students benefit more from specific educator expertise through segregated than integrated services.
b. A principle of service integration is student centeredness, that is, targeting the student as a failure source.
c. Educators should design their curriculum and instruction beginning with appropriate differentiation.
d. Educators should develop curriculum for average students and then adapt it for individual students.

69. The school principal institutes a professional learning community made up of social studies and reading teachers from grades six through eight. This professional learning community is an example of which of the following?

a. Horizontal alignment of curriculum and instruction
b. Vertical alignment of curriculum and instruction
c. Horizontal and vertical alignment of curriculum and instruction
d. Cross-cultural integration of curriculum and instruction

70. Which of the following best represents a mutually beneficial relationship between a school and a community organization?

a. A neighborhood grocery store donates bottled water to the basketball team for home games.
b. The school hosts a clothing drive for a local homeless shelter once a year.
c. A local church has permission to use the school library for meetings on Saturday mornings and the principal is permitted to make announcements to the attendees during the meetings.
d. A medical clinic near the school offers free immunizations and physicals to students actively enrolled at the school.

Constructed Response

1. You are the principal of an 1800-student urban high school with a primarily African-American and Hispanic/Latino student population. The school has an active student newspaper with a much-beloved journalism teacher. Over the past several months, the student-staff have published several items of dubious origin that have caused controversy in the larger community. These items have typically had topics dealing with race relations. You have spoken to the journalism teacher after each incident about not allowing students to publish this type of questionable content. The newest issue of the student newspaper contains another such item. In 150-300 words, describe what you would do to address the situation.

2. You are the new principal of a 700-student elementary (K-5) school. The previous principal left the school in the midst of some controversy and there has been a significant turnover in teaching staff. In your first couple of weeks on the job, you notice a considerable amount of negativity among staff, in large part fomented by teachers who have been at the school for several years and have had multiple principals. In 300-600 words describe the strategies that you would use to address this negativity and change the culture of the school to a more positive tone and improve teacher and staff morale.

3. You are the principal of a school that historically was majority white, non-Hispanic/Latino, non-bilingual. Over the last ten years, the geographical area and your school has experienced a profound change in its demographic makeup. This school year 75% of the student body is Hispanic/Latino, 25% is white (non-Hispanic), and a large number of these are English Language Learners/Bilingual students. The staff of the school is predominately white, not bilingual, and has largely remained unchanged in ethnic makeup from previous year. A significant number of parents have become increasingly upset by what they perceive as a major communication barrier between parents, students, and school teachers/staff. The district superintendent has asked you to develop a new cultural competency program aimed at solving this problem. In 300-600 words, outline the program you would come up with. Include how the program would be implemented and whom the program would include.

Answer Key and Explanations for Test #2

Multiple Choice Questions

1. D: The most appropriate response that the principal can offer the PTO president is that the science curriculum purchase directly supports a school goal. All school resources such as curriculum should be aligned to the school vision and goals. Satisfactory student performance is not an appropriate response given that the school leader may have identified college preparation as an area of improvement, even if students were already meeting expectations in this area. Additionally, the cost of the curriculum is irrelevant if the curriculum is not aligned to the campus vision and goals.

2. D: The collective work of all leaders adds up to more than the sum of its parts (A) in the holistic form of distributed leadership, which emphasizes interdependent leadership (D). One way of describing holistic interdependence is that all members realize they must "sink or swim" together, not individually (C). With this in mind, (A) and (C) are wrong because they refer to the wrong form. Answer (B) is wrong in that in the holistic form, leaders are distinct, but work together.

3. A: According to the National Education Association (NEA), a school acceptable use policy (AUP) should include a preamble explaining need for an AUP; its goals and development; a school conduct code inclusion of online activity; a definition section of important terms; a policy statement of computer services covered and conditions required for student use (e.g., taking a computer responsibility class); an acceptable uses section *and* unacceptable uses section; and a violations and sanctions section, which should tell students how to report policy violations or question policy application (which may conform to the school disciplinary code), not just define violations.

4. D: Behavioral codes of conduct govern student, faculty, staff, and visitor behavior in schools. State regulations typically require schools to give teachers copies upon adoption, send all parents summaries before school years start, and give students copies when school years begin. However, to gain stakeholder buy in and to assure collective understanding and agreement, conduct codes can be developed jointly by parents, teachers, and students.

5. B: Instruction can be differentiated based on content, process, or product. Differentiating instruction based on product means that the teacher provides multiple ways for a student to demonstrate mastery. Allowing students to write an essay gives students an opportunity to demonstrate mastery in written form or in spoken form. Providing students with different versions of assessments is still assessing students using a test and does not constitute differentiated instruction.

6. A: According to some education experts (cf. WestEd.org), school principals and districts surveyed across the United States have reported generally positive impressions of standards-based accountability systems, saying these have improved curriculum and instruction, student assessment practices (C), and student expectations and achievement. However, many districts (over 40%) also reported that teacher morale had been adversely affected by accountability pressures.

7. D: Researchers report that to advocate for excellence and equity in education, successful education leaders follow and recommend giving staff, colleagues, and other learning community members opportunities to develop equity skills. Developing their own equity skills will not automatically spread these through the learning community (A). Successful school leaders study system inequities to discover how they are part of the problems (B) and study equitable leadership characteristics to discover solutions to the problems (C). Additionally, they advise others to develop collaborative approaches across systems (D), enabling exploration of varying perspectives on leadership practices.

8. B: Although professional development (PD) must be job-embedded and school-based, it can occur even outside of the school building if teachers view it as part of their daily work duties and it emerges from and contributes to daily classroom practice. Teachers must be actively involved in the learning process for effective PD. It should be student-centered so that teachers learn to support student learning because PD is not for teachers' own sake. Collaborative teacher problem-solving is a PD guideline because it is valuable, addresses the issue of teacher isolation, and fosters professional and community respect.

9. C: Allowing for variations across states, most public-school districts receive the largest proportion of funding from their state governments. According to the American Association of School Administrators (AASA), the federal government provides between 10 and 20 percent of the funding public school districts receive. Local and intermediate governments combined contributing slightly less than the state government. Only a very small proportion of funding comes from other sources.

10. D: When planning for differentiated instruction, teachers should utilize as much data as possible that can be useful in determining how students can best learn. Identification in special populations such as special education, English as second language, gifted and talented, and others are helpful when planning differentiated instruction but are not the only factors to be considered. Student interests, learning styles, formative and summative data, and other relevant data should all be considered when planning differentiated instruction.

11. B: To evaluate curriculum for cultural and racial equity and improve it as needed, school leaders can instruct teachers to view curriculum as pluralistic and constantly changing to meet changing student populations and needs (A); include multicultural education in the school's curriculum goals (B); not only make sure books contain diversity but also have teachers examine books for prejudiced or discriminatory content (C); and include multicultural education in books, other media, and learning experiences rather than focus it on only foods, festivals, and fun activities (D).

12. C: Student growth is the best data point to inform the principal as to whether the math intervention program was effective and should continue to be funded. Student growth can be calculated by comparing student performance in math at the beginning of the school year to the end of the school year. Although standardized test performance is an important data point, this data alone will not indicate the efficacy of the program, especially for students who may have grown significantly, but not enough to meet standardized test performance requirements.

13. C: Providing teachers with aggregated student data, even in regular intervals, will not likely improve teacher practice. School leaders must disaggregate data to help teachers identify the data that is reflective of their students and their instructional practice. Disaggregated data should also be analyzed in a collaborative process to help identify needs and generate solutions to address those needs.

14. D: Leaders can encourage self-direction in improving among faculty and staff by modeling this behavior. Leaders who are transparent about their own areas of improvement will encourage and set an example for employees. Additionally, the school leader should actively engage employees in self-assessment as well as make resources available for doing so. However, a leader should not leave self-improvement up to employees as it will likely not be done. Employees need support, resources, and encouragement to engage in self-directed improvement.

15. A: Research studies find that, for implementing school-wide technology adoption, required factors are sufficient resources and support, professional development, school structure, school organization, and leadership. Effective professional development must be intentionally and carefully planned, designed with goals in mind, provided continually to keep up with constant changes in the teaching profession, and integrated system-wide or school-wide as part of the school culture through teacher collaboration and sharing of knowledge.

16. B: To foster equity and inclusion in education, school leaders should assure all their teachers develop curriculum and differentiated instruction that are *both* developmentally appropriate *and* culturally diverse; model respect for diversity in their own behaviors, and offer their schools and communities multiple ways for celebrating diversity; involve suitable culturally diverse community stakeholders in school decisions, which *is* their job; and hold all members of their school communities accountable for valuing diversity, equity, and inclusion, not just themselves.

17. A: In diverse communities, school leaders often encounter language barriers when attempting to communicate with parents of students or other community members. While it is helpful when a school leader is fluent in more than one language, there are often a variety of languages that are spoken in these communities. There can be translators, including sign language interpreters, or translation machines available at community meetings when appropriate. There are also many businesses that offer translation services for documents and real-time translation for meetings and conferences.

18. B: In most public school districts, typically the District Office of Achievement and Accountability makes preliminary enrollment projections to inform school budgets. They do not do this alone because of the difficulty of projecting. Instead, they submit their projections to school leaders, who revise them as needed. School leaders do not project their schools' enrollment alone. Final enrollment projections are made by district committees representing not only the Finance and Student Support offices, but also district Achievement and Accountability and Operations offices.

19. D: The best way to get teachers to model for students is for school leaders to model for teachers rather than only talking about it (A). If teaching practices conflict with student cultural beliefs, values, or practices, leaders must instruct teachers to replace or change these, not simply be aware of the conflict (B). Having all teachers know a few words or phrases in each student's first language (L1) makes classrooms welcoming, psychologically safe learning environments (C). Similarly, leaders should ensure all staff members learn to pronounce students' names correctly (D).

20. D: A primary aspect of implementing a school improvement plan is to use data to assess goal progress and completion. Integrating technology tools to accomplish this can improve the ease at which school improvement progress can be measured and improve the timeliness and accuracy of response to progress checks. Utilizing technology in other areas such as to facilitate collaboration, administer assessments, and communicate with stakeholders are valuable; however, utilizing technology to collect, organize, and analyze data for school improvement and progress monitoring is most closely related to the implementation of the school improvement plan.

21. B: Empirical research into effective practices improving schools and student achievement finds that school leaders overcame resistance to change through proactive strategies, including owning and demonstrating continuing commitment, establishing supportive administrative networks, establishing priorities for change, and communicating with others more intentionally.

22. C: Students designing digital storybooks is the best example of creating content using digital media. It is beneficial for students to access information using technology, such as visiting wiki pages. Students can also curate content that already exists, such as gathering photos from the web. However, creating content using digital media empowers students to use technology at the highest level of Bloom's taxonomy.

23. A: Formative data helps teachers to assess their effectiveness during instruction (rather than after) and accordingly make adjustments to improve student outcomes. Summative data can assist teachers in identifying areas of improvement in their teaching practice but is often too late to identify specific remedial student groups. Student profiles from permanent records (e.g., demographics, assessment histories, family information, etc.) provide less detailed information to inform instruction. Enrollment data helps educators identify budgetary needs and student demographic distributions, but do not inform instruction, staff development, remedial student groups, or information plans.

24. D: When school visions are developed through collaboration among employees, they tend to be more appropriate to the contexts of their local school districts, which is an advantage. Collaboratively developed school visions typically are *not* implemented as quickly as those personally developed by school leaders, which also tend to be clearer and more coherent than those developed collaboratively. Collaboratively developed school visions do take longer to develop, slowing change, which is a disadvantage, not an advantage.

25. B: Traditional methods of assessment usually involve a standardized test with closed questions that require students to select an answer from several choices. Authentic assessment allows students to demonstrate mastery of content and objectives in different ways within the context of the subject matter. This may include project assessments, writing assessments, and performance assessment. The goal of authentic assessment is to provide students with the opportunity to authentically demonstrate that they have mastered the content.

26. A: Before engaging any community resource, school leaders must consider whether it is compatible with the school's vision and mission. Some resources may have impact in the long-term rather than immediately and should not be discarded because effects will not be seen immediately. Additionally, as communities develop, new resources may be made available. Not all available resources will have a history of prior implementation but may prove beneficial for student learning. Similarly, as the school builds new partnerships, community resources may become available through new community relationships.

27. A: Vision and goals are deemed appropriate when they are based on multiple sources of data that reflect current practice. It is important for school leaders to solicit buy in from community members, but this is not an indicator of the appropriateness of the goals. Additionally, the school vision and goals can leverage school strengths, but areas of deficit or weakness are often addressed in the goals. Although schools may have similar demographics and performance history, the school vision and goals should be based upon a thorough analysis of the data unique to the campus. Consequently, the vision and goals of schools may differ even though the performance history and demographics of the school may appear to be similar.

28. D: Teachers are more receptive to principal feedback that is not unexpected (A): principals should tell teachers their expectations and encourage teachers to establish goals before offering feedback related to these (B). As behaviorism has shown, effective feedback is immediate, not delayed (C). Effective feedback strategies include identifying teacher strengths first and then communicating criticisms in the form of requesting solutions (D).

29. D: The principal should take action that allows stakeholders to participate in the process of refocusing attention to campus vision and goals. A community meeting would allow for two-way communication so that the principal can hear the concerns of the community and so that the community can hear about the alignment of the program to the campus vision and goals.

30. C: To address weak areas, it is better to implement strategies that are backed by research and have been proven to yield good results. This can save the campus the time, effort, and resources that would be wasted if untested and unproven strategies were implemented unsuccessfully. When a leader is looking for strategies to foster change on campus, using research-based and proven best practices is beneficial because there will be a clear direction as to how to successfully implement the strategy and a realistic idea of what results to expect. When untested strategies are implemented, the outcome is less certain. Untested strategies also often take more research and a process of trial and error, or a learning curve, to implement, both of which can delay the implementation of change.

31. C: School leaders and others should analyze school data based upon formative classroom assessments and standardized state summative assessments. The data analyzed should include data across grade levels, across school years, by subjects, by student cohorts, by student special populations, and by individual teachers, when possible. Analysis of data should be holistic in order to identify school strengths, needs for improvement, and trends to properly inform the school vision and mission.

32. C: Curriculum and instruction must be aligned to assessment because what is taught must be measured and what is measured must be taught. If instruction is not aligned to the assessment, it is likely that there will be no measurement of how well students mastered what was taught. Additionally, if instruction is not aligned to the assessment, it is likely that students will be assessed on concepts and material that they have not been taught. Neither of the scenarios is fair or beneficial to students.

33. C: All of these questions are important to consider when developing school goals. However, aligning the school goals to the school vision is most critical. The school vision describes how the school is envisioned to be in the future and the school goals are the steps that will enable the school to accomplish that vision.

34. A: Leaders should use as many opportunities as possible to observe staff performance in order to have a well-rounded view of their performance. The opportunities may include various days of the week, times of the day, and varied circumstances. A leader should be intentional and deliberate about seeking different opportunities to observe staff at a variety of times in a variety of circumstances in order to obtain a fair and holistic view of staff performance.

35. B: Research from Stanford University (Grissom, Loeb, and Master, 2013) into effective school leader use of instructional time finds that improvements in student achievement are predicted by time spent on evaluation of teachers and/or curriculum, coaching teachers, and developing the school education program. It is *not* predicted in informal classroom walkthroughs, particularly in high schools. The investigators speculate this may be because school leaders frequently do not incorporate walkthroughs into broader strategies for school improvement.

36. D: A coach is a professional who helps a teacher develop the skills necessary to do their job effectively. A coach is a staff member who does not supervise or evaluate the person being coached. This helps to foster a relationship of trust between the coach and the teacher. A coach will identify a teacher's areas of strength and weakness based on a predetermined rubric or set of expectations. Then the coach will provide one-on-one support to the teacher to help improve targeted areas. A coach may provide books and resources, recommend professional development sessions, model effective teaching methods, observe the teacher in practice to provide real-time feedback, assist in the lesson planning process, and guide the teacher in self-reflection and critical analysis processes. A coach provides individualized, targeted support to teachers and helps them to grow, usually in a shorter period of time than other forms of professional development support.

37. A: State funding under Title I and Smart Start legislation is often available as a way for school leaders to hire school parent facilitators, whose jobs are to involve families in their children's educations. School leaders should not always expect for parents to visit the school. Instead, school leaders should also be visible in the community to facilitate family involvement. School leaders can develop community relationships by beginning with parents who are already involved, but make an effort to involve parents who have not been previously involved. Fostering parental involvement requires two-way communication, not just one-way communication such as robocalls or newsletters.

38. C: Obeying federal, state, and local laws and regulations (II) and implementing the local board of education's administrative regulations and policies (V) could both conflict with acting to change laws and regulations that are against valid education goals (IV), or vice versa, as obeying and implementing laws, regulations, and policies can be countermanded by acting to change laws, regulations, or policies.

39. B: The principal should consider the campus vision and goals when determining how to allocate resources, including technology resources. The first step that a principal should take when considering spending school funds is determining how the purchase will support the achievement of the vision and goals. When considering upgrading or replacing technology, it is appropriate for the principal to evaluate the current condition of the technology or seek ways to save money; however, the first step that should be taken is to determine if the spending is in alignment with the school goals and vision.

40. A: In many American communities and states, schools provide the chief—and often the only—mental health (MH) services that children receive. Parents are more comfortable with such services when they are provided in familiar school settings by familiar staff, rather than avoiding them. Research studies find students are *more* likely to seek counseling services in schools than to look elsewhere. Another reason for school-community collaboration is the necessity of coordinating school and community MH services, not separating them.

41. D: The term decentralization refers to the transfer of power and authority from the school districts to principals to make decisions related to budgets and staffing. In centralized school districts, the central office determines campus spending and the principal has little to no control over how funds are used. In decentralized school districts, principals have greater control over how to use the funds allotted to their school campus.

42. A: Research conducted over recent decades finds that although socioeconomic status (SES) correlates strongly with student academic achievement, both available school resources and school curriculum correlate even more strongly with student achievement than SES. Researchers say these findings should motivate school leaders and schools to reduce achievement gaps rather than blame them on family or community SES.

43. D: One of the foundations of a professional learning community is identifying the standards and curriculum that must be taught and ensuring that the curriculum is delivered effectively. A question that PLC members must ask is "What do we want students to learn?". Answering this question ensures that the standards-based curriculum is prioritized, and that formative and summative assessment is a reflection of the curriculum that is taught.

44. D: In SPBS programs, tier 3 is for the small proportion of students not responding to tier 1 or tier 2 interventions. It involves intensive, individualized interventions tailored to each student. Small socio-emotional group instruction in social and emotional skills, daily student check-in and check-out procedures, and enlisting family support for small-group intervention and instruction are all techniques associated with tier 2.

45. B: Given that students were consistently performing well in math with the exception of three specific math objectives indicates that there is an issue with the curriculum being used to teach those objectives. Factors such as teacher quality or biased assessments would negatively impact student performance in all objectives, not just a select few and performance would vary from student to student. The most likely reason for students consistently underperforming in the same area despite being taught by different teachers is a misalignment of curriculum to the assessment of the objectives.

46. B: According to researchers (Mitchell and Sackney, 1998), both reflection (i.e., considering their own practices) and conversation (i.e., discussing their and colleagues' practices) enable teachers to have awareness of their own and others' practices, evaluate them, and discover possible alternatives. These are cognitive processes. Affirmation of one another as professionals, and invitation into school decision-making both validate all staff members' contributions, acknowledge individual professional competencies, and thereby establish positive working relationships. These are affective processes.

47. C: Buy in from internal and external community members would be the most likely strategy for engaging stakeholders in the implementation of the school vision and goals. Buy in is achieved when stakeholders are included in the process of developing the school vision and goals. When stakeholders are part of the process, they are more likely to feel ownership of the product which motivates them to engage in implementation. Communicating the school vision and goals to the community is important, but it may not lead to engagement in implementation if stakeholders do not feel that they were including in the process of developing the vision and goals.

48. C: Cross-curricular instruction is the deliberate making of connections between various content areas so that students may apply their knowledge in more than one content area at a time. For example, students may examine the historical setting of a story in a reading class, utilize math strategies in a science class, or discuss geometric principles in an art class. Cross-curricular instruction is beneficial for students because it demonstrates the relevance of their content knowledge.

49. D: Of the choices presented, choice D is the most valid. Leaders should seek to share substantial academic gains with the community with regularity to try to capture the attention and support of families and entities, such as businesses, in the community. The other options are not very generalizable or necessarily relevant to school goals in general, so they are not as applicable to the scenario.

50. D: All of these factors are important to consider, but the leader must first ensure that the professional development will help staff meet the vision and goals that have already been established. A leader needs to be deliberate in selecting professional development for staff members so that the professional development is purposeful in helping staff achieve the campus goals and vision.

51. A: The components of an effective plan include action steps, persons responsible, time frames, milestones, resources needed, and evidence of implementation. The plan will include the resources needed to accomplish the plan so that these resources are planned for and obtained, thus preventing delay in the plan's accomplishment. The evidence of implementation should be included in the plan so that ongoing monitoring can take place. Depending on the aspect of the plan, evidence of implementation could include documents, visible indicators, or regular meetings.

52. A: The logistics function of the ICS identifies services and resources for supporting incident response needs. The planning function collects and evaluates information, identifies incident response issues, develops action plans, and recommends future actions. The command function manages incidents overall and is directly responsible for public safety, information, and community response agency liaisons. The operations function develops objectives, organizes resources, and directs actions and resources for incident responses.

53. A: Summative assessment is assessment that is used to evaluate student learning for mastery. Summative assessment usually occurs at the end of an instructional unit or a designated period of time, such as a grading period or school year. These assessments are aligned to objectives or standards and are usually high stakes, which means they may count for a significant grade or may determine a student's progress in their educational career. A summative assessment may be a midterm or final exam, a research project, a unit test, or a standardized exam. The results of summative assessments may determine a student's grade promotion or earning of course credit. Results from summative assessments may also determine a school's performance according to accountability standards. Summative assessment results are often used by school leaders for instructional planning and goal setting for the subsequent school year.

54. A: An emotionally safe environment is an environment where everyone can learn. It is free from all obstacles, negative emotions, and conflicts due to preventative strategies and quick resolutions. When an environment is not emotionally safe, children can feel fear, anxiety, and a host of other negative emotions. In an emotionally safe environment, both adults and children feel comfortable participating in the learning environment and interacting with one another. There is an absence of peer-to-peer conflict, peer-to-adult conflict, and bullying.

55. B: The principal noted that they were not able to implement plans properly because they did not have time. Action items in the plan were not accomplished, indicating that this is a time management issue and the leader needs to set appropriate priorities for accomplishing tasks. Simply adding hours to one's work week does not mean that those hours will be spent completing the right tasks. School leaders must become efficient at prioritizing their activities to achieve school goals. Additionally, the leader is concerned with self-improvement, so holding others accountable is not an appropriate solution in this instance.

56. A: Teachers and staff have more buy in when changes are made if they are part of the process. Creating a committee that does not include school leadership demonstrates the leader's willingness to give authority to the staff to promote change and a willingness to accept changes that are not generated by leadership. Suggestion boxes and town hall meetings allow staff to share ideas, but these ideas still must be vetted by the school leader as a gate keeper and may not fully address the school's current culture. Teacher engagement in the Shared Decision-Making Committee is vital for school success but will not likely address a campus-wide perception of top-down leadership.

57. D: To mobilize and develop community school support, school leaders should consider that businesses and community-based organizations use different language than educators, and should learn and speak their languages accordingly. School leaders must not only exchange their visions, missions, wants, and needs with those of prospective community partners and identify where these match, they must moreover identify where they overlap, i.e., shared commonalities despite differences. School leaders must show prospective partners how collaboration benefits them. Potential partners have motivations as varied as the community organizations interested in collaborating with schools.

58. C: Professional learning communities allow staff with shared roles or responsibilities to collaborate in a way that meets the needs of teachers and students. These communities are usually goal-driven and encourage the sharing of ideas and responsibilities. Professional learning communities are used in a variety of ways, but the primary purpose is to facilitate collaboration among educators.

59. D: Measurable goals can be quantified, and non-measurable goals cannot be quantified. This goal is measurable because calculating the percentage of students who earned at least a B average in their math class can reveal whether or not the goal was met. It also identifies how students are expected to perform in order to reach the goal. When goals are measurable, it is easy to determine whether or not the goal has been met.

60. C: Developing a school safety plan requires participation by the entire community because schools with the most numerous and severe violence and crime incidents are in communities with the same characteristics. School leaders and staff are not the only ones (A) because addressing community issues reflected in schools requires collaboration among resources contributing varied expertise and because schools are for learning, not controlling (B) violence or crime. Not only law enforcement and mental health personnel (D) but also parents, community leaders, business leaders, and other community professionals serving youth should participate as well as students, teachers, and administrators.

61. B: Research finds that school leader participation in PD is what determines teacher and school-wide participation in PD. School leaders set an example for teachers by actively engaging in the PD that teachers are expected to engage in. School leaders should have a vision for PD offerings but can empower teachers to choose PD offerings that meet their needs. School leaders can facilitate PD activities but should also allow teacher leaders to facilitate PD as well. School leaders should monitor implementation of PD but this activity is not directly related to being a role model for teachers.

62. D: An effective school leader is transparent when making decisions. This transparency includes sharing data and/or rationale for making decisions. The school leader has already determined that the fine arts program should be discontinued so the best action for the principal to take next is to explain the rationale for that decision to the school community.

63. A: A school must hold a Manifestation Determination Review within 10 school days according to the following criteria: if the school is seeking to change student placement for more than 10 consecutive days for disciplinary reasons; if the school suspends a student for disciplinary reasons for more than 10 cumulative days that form a pattern; the school is deciding to expel or otherwise exclude a student for disciplinary reasons; or the school convenes this meeting after a disciplinary incident.

64. D: The Incident Command System (ICS) planning (A) function collects and evaluates data, identifies issues, develops action plans, and recommends future actions. The logistics (B) function identifies services and resources needed to support incident response needs. The command (C) function is responsible for overall incident management, public safety, information, and community agency liaisons. The operations (D) function develops objectives, organizes resources, and directs resources and actions to incident response. (The other ICS function is finance.)

65. B: While staying informed of new trends and technology is useful in this role, it is not central to the actual implementation of a new technology that is in its early implementation. Change management often requires more direct support of a wide range of needs from staff and students. Demonstrating the use of the technology (choice A), setting expectations and encouraging effort (choice C), and helping with implementation (choice D) all are a more direct way the school leader should help to implement change in this situation. Both question and answer are highlighted.

66. A: Classroom observations, student class grades, and summative assessment data would be the best sources of data to provide feedback to teachers to improve student learning. Data sources for improving teaching and learning should include instructional delivery (classroom observations) and student performance outcomes. Both formative and summative assessment data can be used to determine student mastery of objectives and efficacy of instructional delivery.

67. C: School leaders should frequently highlight successes related to accomplishing the school vision to show stakeholders that the vision is viable and successful. Ceremonies for celebrating successes and other ways of highlighting successes are beneficial but must be conducted frequently in order to change a negative school culture. Providing professional development for teachers related to culture can be beneficial but would not address issues with culture for all employees on campus. Additionally, it is important for leaders to make observations about school culture, but observations without action will not positively impact school culture.

68. C: Researchers have found segregated services more likely to cause isolated skill development and fragmentation, whereas integrated comprehensive services require cross-disciplinary sharing of specific educator expertise, benefiting students (A) and colleagues alike. Although its staff design must be student based, a principle underlying integrated comprehensive services is that the source of student failure is the system, not the student (B). School leaders and other educators integrating services should design curriculum and instruction beginning with differentiation (C) rather than adapt it afterward (D).

69. C: The PLC will include teachers in the same grade level in different subjects which is horizontal alignment. The PLC will also include teachers in different grade levels in the same subject which is vertical alignment. Consequently, this PLC is an example of both horizontal and vertical alignment of curriculum and instruction.

70. C: This scenario best represents a mutually beneficial relationship. The church has the benefit of having a meeting place and the principal has the benefit of communicating directly with community members on a regular basis. The other activities help to build positive relationships between the school and the community, but are one-sided.

Constructed Response

1. Essay question graders commonly look for the following elements in a strong response: strong content knowledge, clear organization, and effective arguments or examples. Language and usage are not usually strictly graded, but can make a big impact on the clarity of your ideas.

Please use the provided rubric to make sure your response meets these common criteria. Try to have a friend or family member grade your response for you or take a break after writing your response and return to grade it with fresh eyes.

Constructed Response Rubric

Domain	Description
Content Knowledge	• The response directly addresses every part of the prompt. • The response demonstrates independent knowledge of the topic. • The response discusses the topic at an appropriate depth.
Organization	• The response introduces the topic, usually with a thesis statement or by restating the prompt. • The response directly addresses the prompt by providing a clear and concise answer or solution. • The answer or solution is supported by logical arguments or evidence. • The response restates the main idea in the conclusion.
Arguments and Examples	• The response provides a reasonable answer to the prompt. • The answer is supported by strong reasoning or evidence. • The response develops ideas logically and connects ideas to one another. • The reasoning and evidence provided act to support a unified main idea.
Language and Usage	• The response demonstrates effective use of grammar and uses varied sentence structure throughout the response. • The response demonstrates correct use of spelling, punctuation, and capitalization. • The response demonstrates strong and varied use of vocabulary relevant to the topic and appropriate for the intended audience.

2. Essay question graders commonly look for the following elements in a strong response: strong content knowledge, clear organization, and effective arguments or examples. Language and usage are not usually strictly graded, but can make a big impact on the clarity of your ideas.

Please use the provided rubric to make sure your response meets these common criteria. Try to have a friend or family member grade your response for you or take a break after writing your response and return to grade it with fresh eyes.

CONSTRUCTED RESPONSE RUBRIC

Domain	Description
Content Knowledge	• The response directly addresses every part of the prompt. • The response demonstrates independent knowledge of the topic. • The response discusses the topic at an appropriate depth.
Organization	• The response introduces the topic, usually with a thesis statement or by restating the prompt. • The response directly addresses the prompt by providing a clear and concise answer or solution. • The answer or solution is supported by logical arguments or evidence. • The response restates the main idea in the conclusion.
Arguments and Examples	• The response provides a reasonable answer to the prompt. • The answer is supported by strong reasoning or evidence. • The response develops ideas logically and connects ideas to one another. • The reasoning and evidence provided act to support a unified main idea.
Language and Usage	• The response demonstrates effective use of grammar and uses varied sentence structure throughout the response. • The response demonstrates correct use of spelling, punctuation, and capitalization. • The response demonstrates strong and varied use of vocabulary relevant to the topic and appropriate for the intended audience.

3. Essay question graders commonly look for the following elements in a strong response: strong content knowledge, clear organization, and effective arguments or examples. Language and usage are not usually strictly graded, but can make a big impact on the clarity of your ideas.

Please use the provided rubric to make sure your response meets these common criteria. Try to have a friend or family member grade your response for you or take a break after writing your response and return to grade it with fresh eyes.

CONSTRUCTED RESPONSE RUBRIC

Domain	Description
Content Knowledge	• The response directly addresses every part of the prompt. • The response demonstrates independent knowledge of the topic. • The response discusses the topic at an appropriate depth.
Organization	• The response introduces the topic, usually with a thesis statement or by restating the prompt. • The response directly addresses the prompt by providing a clear and concise answer or solution. • The answer or solution is supported by logical arguments or evidence. • The response restates the main idea in the conclusion.
Arguments and Examples	• The response provides a reasonable answer to the prompt. • The answer is supported by strong reasoning or evidence. • The response develops ideas logically and connects ideas to one another. • The reasoning and evidence provided act to support a unified main idea.
Language and Usage	• The response demonstrates effective use of grammar and uses varied sentence structure throughout the response. • The response demonstrates correct use of spelling, punctuation, and capitalization. • The response demonstrates strong and varied use of vocabulary relevant to the topic and appropriate for the intended audience.